DIVERSIFIED MONEY AND EXTERNAL DEBT

DIVERSIFIED MONEY AND EXTERNAL DEBT

A Model for the United States

Ivan Ovcaricek-Rostok

Strategic Book Publishing and Rights Co.

Strategic Book Publishing & Rights Co., LLC
www.sbpra.net

For information about special discounts for bulk purchases, please contact Strategic Book Publishing and Rights Co. Special Sales, at bookorder@sbpra.net.

ISBN: 978-1-948858-23-6

DECLARATION

Type of work	Research work
Type of research	Conceptual research
Subject of elaboration	Financial debt of the state
Subject of Research	The United States
Researcher	Dr. Sc. Ivan Ovčariček-Rostok
Treatment of research subject	Financial and Economic
Publication of the Research	Book Format
Country of the research publication	The United States
Registration of the work	The United States
Editing of the text Graphic-art formatting Press	SBPRA, Houston
Promotion and distribution	SBPRA, Houston
Area where selling the book is allowed	The United States
Copyright holder	Dr. Sc. Ivan Ovčariček-Rostok
The Right to Sell Copyright and Research Results	Dr. Sc. Ivan Ovčariček-Rostok

RESEARCH RESULTS

Financial effect for the US through 10 years	Preventing future growth of external debt $ 31,567,931,000,000 Reducing Interest Cost to Debt $ 6,224,341,000,000 Supplementary annual GDP growth $ 15,684,063,000,000

Publication of this work publication, including in E-format, is not permitted outside the US territory.

Acknowledgements

I express my gratitude to the people from SBPRA who were included in the publication of this book, especially Mrs. Lynn Eddy, Mrs. Ellen Green, Mr. Robert Fletcher, and Mr. Bruce Martin.

The United States has entered a long-term economic deviation of its external debt, which was $21,122,000,000,000 on 11.04.2018. Stopping and reducing this debt can only be initiated by the current US president.

The concept of this work will show three potential benefits for the United States over the next ten years:

- *Prevent further growth of the external debt by $ 31,567,931,000,000*
- *Cut interest charges on external debt by $6,224,341,000,000*
- *Eliminating the growth of imports, resulting in an annual growth of the GDP of $15,684,063,000,000*

Table of Contents

Preface

This research has only one goal: the rationalization of the growing external debt of the United States, which has the greatest impact on the world economy.

In the analysis of the debt problem, historical data were used so as not to hurt one's current economic interest.

If we start with the fact that the external debt of the US in 2013 was 31.27 percent of all external debts in the world, it can be concluded that it is the world's biggest economic problem. This should not be neglected by the politicians, who are largely unaware of the size of the economic problem. It is not known whether there is an understanding of how big this problem is in the United States, which means that no one knows who can solve it, when to start, and how to accomplish it.

This work gives conceptual answers to these questions. The problem is an economic monstrosity that needs to be urgently restrained, because the US has already entered a state of economic collapse. It can no longer pay for its final consumption, therefore continually increasing external debt.

The answer to the first question, who can start solving this problem, is the current president of the United States.

The answer to the second question, when to begin solving this problem, is immediately.

The answer to the third question, how to solve this problem, is the application of the category of diversified money in US foreign trade.

To get started, it is first necessary to get the right to use the method called "the category of diversified money" from its author. Then, the compilation and design of a project for the practical inclusion of the category of diversified money into the financial and trading system of the US should be started.

Diversified money is the universal lever to achieve rationalization of external debt.

To solve the problem of the United States' current large external debt, it is not appropriate to introduce customs duties on certain types of merchandise goods, as this provokes the misunderstanding of other countries, which then leads to a series of world political and economic conflicts. In addition, introducing customs is the method used in the twentieth century. The new method should be economically civilized and objective.

To solve the current international economic problems, it is necessary to accept the principles of economic fairness in foreign trade through the syntagma of "spend as much as you have" and "do not take from future generations," which is ensured by the introduction of the method of the category of diversified money. This method is protection against the unfair exploitation of other economic spaces.

Introduction

The text of this work is the application and partial compilation of earlier research texts by the author:

- *The Economic Success of a State: The Principle of the Economic Duals and the Category of Diversified Money*
- *Debt of the State and the Danger of Economic Collapse*
- *Optimum in the Economics of a State*
- *The Gold Money Constant and Entrepreneurship*

The above-mentioned books deal with the theme of economic success of the state. The new processing refers to the specialization of the research, which is particularly related to the problem of the purchasing power and the external debt of the United States, the most important global economic entity.

The purchasing power of the economic space of the US is the largest economic resource in the world that, free of charge, is used and exploited by a large number of partner countries. The use of this purchasing power should be in reciprocity in value with the purchasing power of its partner states. External trade without balance is not fair. This reciprocal balance should be the basic principle of US foreign trade. This problem needs to be addressed immediately, which will allow the US to achieve ultimate economic balance with its partner countries within twenty years. The problem has already escalated so much that it now threatens a serious global economic deviation of destructive proportions. The first major victim of this deviation could in fact be the US economy, which would have a devastating impact on countries that get business resources from this economic space.

Solving the big US foreign debt problem can have two phases: The first is simply stopping the growth of the external debt, and the second is to reduce that external debt. For both, it is necessary to introduce the category of diversified money.

Stopping External Debt Growth

The first step in rationalizing the external debt of the US is to begin stopping its growth, which is growing annually and has existed since 1961. This dynamic is connected with each presidential electoral period.

In general terms, external indebtedness in its first stage brings beneficial effects to the state. There seems to be economic growth or development, as well as raising the living standards of the population. If the debt is not used to strengthen the productive power of the state in the second phase, then problems arise when the debt is to be repaid. At that point, growth or development begins to slow down, and the population's standard of living decreases. There are two solutions to this: The first is using a new loan to settle old obligations, and the other is to begin printing money, thus masking the problem.

Considering this problem for the United States, it can be concluded that stopping the indebtedness of the state would cause problems, as the debt was not used to strengthen the state's economic power, but rather to increase final consumption, which does not have a reverse financial effect.

Reducing External Debt

The second stage in rationalizing the external debt of the state is to stop its growth and reduce its height. This is a more difficult task than simply stopping its growth. The reason for this is that previous economic conditions must be created. The growth of the economic performance of the state in the form of savings and higher prices of consumer goods is assumed. Such an organization of the state provokes reactions and political dissatisfaction, as well as various demonstrations of this dissatisfaction. Then, political manipulation is primarily used to correct the problem. Starting in 1961, US presidents have not been willing to stop the chain growth of the external debt or achieve its reduction. However, now is the time when this must be done.

Lack of Equilibrium in the Economic Space

The US now has the problem of the successful economic management of the state as an economic space. The reason for this is that there are no precisely defined and elaborate economic principles on which to achieve this in an optimal way. Concepts are the principles that make up the framework for the behavior of the people who make political decisions. If such principles are explicitly set up, many political misunderstandings can be avoided.

The first major problem that exists today in US economics is the steady rise of the external debt that needs to be repaid. There is now a problem when it comes to investment spending, which has its own return capacity, but if its final consumption does not have a return capacity, then that's a serious problem. Poor debt policy leads to impoverishment of the population.

Increase in final consumption generated by debt produces the equivalent of tomorrow's spending cuts when the debt is repaid. This shift of tomorrow's purchasing power to some present time is stealing from tomorrow's generation of people. A further major problem in the US is the erosion of the value of money, degrading its third function, which is the deposit of value.

Framework for Solving Economic Problems

The problem of the external debt of the US can be solved by exploring and optimizing three basic categories: The first is the stability of money as the equivalent of all usable goods in material and immaterial form; the second is entrepreneurship as a driving force that creates usable goods; the third is the economic policy that regulates relationships. Without these three complex elements and the application of the category of diversified money, there is no solution to the country's external debt problem.

Money is not a direct and concrete usable good; it is an ideal and a mirror, and entrepreneurship is the creator of usable goods. It's an art. Money and entrepreneurship are two categories that are linked to each other. Like with living creatures, money can be considered the blood and entrepreneurial power as the heart, which draws the blood into the body and ensures life. Money in the state secures life for the population, and entrepreneurial power drives it through the economic body (the state). There we need to be very careful. If you put too much blood into the body, it will have high blood pressure and become deformed and sick. If you pump too little blood, anemia and weakness arise. Nature teaches us this lesson.

Purpose of the Research

The purpose of this research is to acquire a certain quantum of knowledge that can be useful for US economics. Good application of ideas and conclusions from this paper can bring financial benefits to the US, amounting to more than a trillion dollars per year. It is a task for almost two generations of people. For this reason, the US should accept the idea of redeeming the right of using the category of diversified money as a method for rationalizing the external debt.

Chapter 1

Deviations in Economic Security

1. The Economic Security Problem

The economic security of the United States has been significantly reduced over the last 38 years. This is a high-risk economic deviation. It is shown in two forms: The first is shown in Table 1 and is expressed in the form of a series of economic security quotients; the second form is shown in Table 2 and is expressed by the average annual growth of the external debt over the period of nine presidents. It also shows the constant accumulation of the external debt.

This huge debt was accumulated because there was no adequate policy of state economic security. Moreover, the state did not have a method at its disposal that would enable it. The accumulated debt is now so large that it will take about twenty years for its depreciation, if the appropriate conceptual basis is provided.

Economic security is the foundation of all other security.

Table 1: Growth rate of the gross domestic product and grow rate of the foreign debt through presidential periods.

Election Period	President	The Rate of Growth of the Gross Domestic Product (%)	The Average Rate of Growth of the Foreign Debt (%)	Quotient of Economical Security (3:4)
1	2	3	4	5
1961–1969	J. F. Kennedy and L. B. Johnson	39.6	29.6	1.34
1969–1977	R. M. Nixon and G. R. Ford	22.1	112.2	0.20
1977–1981	J. E. Carter, Jr.	13.2	11.0	1.20
1981–1989	R. W. Reagan	30.0	130.32	0.23
1989–1993	G. H. W. Bush	9.1	46.7	0.19
1993–2001	W. J. Clinton	31.0	85.0	0.27
2001–2009	G. W. Bush	14.4	142.7	0.10
2009–2017	B. Obama	12.2	47.04	0.26
2017–2019	D. Trump	2.3 7.9	5.40	1.46
Average of economical safety		**20.08**	**67.77**	**0.30**

Note: The minimum value of the economic security quotient of the state is one (1.00)

Table 2: Dynamics of external debt through presidential periods.

Election Period	President	Debt at the Beginning of Mandate (billion)	Debt at the End of Mandate (billion)	The Average Annual Growth of Debt (%) (4-3):N:3 *
1	2	3	4	5
1961–1969	J. F. Kennedy and L. B. Johnson	297	385	3.7
1969–1977	R. M. Nixon and G. R. Ford	385	817	14.0
1977–1981	J. E. Carter	817	907	2.8
1981–1989	R. W. Reagan	907	2.089	16.3
1989–1993	G. H. W. Bush	2.089	3.065	11.7
1993–2001	W. J. Clinton	3.065	5.674	10.6
2001–2009	G. W. Bush	5.674	13.768	17.8
2009–2017	B. Obama	13.768	20.245	5.9
2017–2019	D. Trump	20.245	21.355	2.7
Average of the growth rate of the debt				**9.5**

*N = number of years

Note: The optimal growth value of the external debt of the state is zero (0.00).

2. Solving Economic Security Problems

Solving the problem of economic security has two phases: The first is to stop further debt increases, and the second is the repayment of the debt. To solve this problem, the foreign trade and financial system of the state must introduce diversified money. Diversified money stops further growth of the debt, and the diversification is the source of innovation for the repayment of external debt.

The method of diversifying money starts with several principles. These are:

- Import of goods should be paid by diversified money
- The exchange rate of the diversified money is determined on the basis of the ratio of the value of exports and imports of each month to each individual country
- Diversified money is being redeemed by a domestic business bank
- Foreign exchange differences from the sale of diversified money belong to the state.

This method is elaborated in a separate chapter.

There are three assumptions needed to solve the problem of economic security:

1. The state has enough economic potential
2. The competence of the executive authority

3. That diversified money has been introduced into foreign trade and the state's financial system

The United States can satisfy all three of these assumptions.

Chapter 2

Economic Potential of the State

The United States is among the world's best in regard to the economic and living standards of its citizens. There are many factors that have enabled such a condition: an abundance of space; a favorable climate; favorable conditions for agriculture; huge mineral wealth; numerous, diverse and well-educated people; long-term independence; an extended period without war within its borders; no period of feudalism; a very strong union movement; great capital; and a stable democratic system and market economy, where the democratic changes of political parties in power do not greatly affect economic development and the standard of living.

The basis of the US economy is the free market and entrepreneurship, where business decisions are made in line with market expectations and needs. State influence is felt in the macroeconomic interest-rate policy and the like. A favorable framework for economic development is the positive laws that have long been in force, such as anti-monopolistic laws that do not allow a single company to monopolize production and determine price. The laws protect consumers from low-quality and bad goods, the workers from bad working conditions, and the environment from excessive pollution. Funds are taken from the state budget for research and development of various industries and products that help numerous regions and cities achieve a greater degree of development.

In the US, a relatively small part of the population, about 2.7 percent, deals with agriculture, yet it is among the most productive in the world. It is marked by great estates, very modern mechanization and chemical-technical protection, and is stimulated by the great internal market and the worldwide political and economic connections where the surpluses are being sold. Almost everything is produced in the country, and production is divided into sectors according to climatic conditions. At the far subtropical southeast of Florida, citrus fruits are produced, and in the south cotton, tobacco, and soy. On the vast plains, from the Appalachians to the Rocky Mountains, corn and wheat are sown, which are used for the nutrition of a large number of cattle in the Great Lakes area, where Chicago's largest slaughterhouse is located. In the northeast are significant dairy production and fruit growing. Dry and mountainous areas in the west are unsuitable for agriculture, and the sheltered valleys in the far west grow fruits and vegetables. The naturally dry California Valley is constantly irrigated.

The secondary sector is comprised of 23.9 percent of working Americans. The US produces and consumes the most energy in the world. There are large oil fields in Texas, California, and Alaska, and coal in the Appalachians. Large natural gas deposits are along the Gulf of Mexico, and most of the rivers have been used to generate electricity. Thirty dams were built on the Tennessee River alone.

The US also has the largest nuclear power infrastructure, using uranium stocks in Colorado. In such a large and geologically diverse area, all the required minerals are processed in a powerful industry. The US did not begin the industrial revolution, but the invention of the moving band helped to innovate later industrial production in the world.

The industry has developed strongly thanks to the rich resources of energy, raw materials, and numerous and well-educated people. Almost everything is produced in modern industrial plants, including world-famous American products like cars, computers, aircraft, telephones, etc. Three industrial regions stand out: The Northeast, the Gulf of Mexico, and the Pacific Industrial Region. Today's industry has fewer employees and more and more machines, robots, and automation. However, although US industry produces large quantities of goods, the country is a bigger importer of industrial products than exporter, creating an enormous trade deficit.

Most US residents (73.5 percent) work in tertiary activities, of which scientific research is the most significant. The largest worldwide concentration of research laboratories and scientists is in the so-called Silicon Valley. American financial companies and retail stores are also some of the world's most significant. The Hollywood film industry is without competition in the world and generates huge profits.

Source: Wikipedia

Chapter 3

Competence of the Executive

In order to start solving the problem of the huge US external debt, a competent executive government, which can generate the appropriate economic policy, is needed. The head of the executive branch of government in the US is the president. The current president is certainly competent enough to address this problem. He has practical economic experience, knowledge, understanding of the gravity of this problem, and the courage to make a positive step in line with his pre-election platform. The president of the United States is the head of state, the supreme executive power authority. He can affect the state's economy by proposing and making regulatory decisions. This also applies to those decisions related to exports, imports, and payment regulations.

The idealistic policy of free-world trade has brought the US to the brink of financial collapse. Over a period of 57 years, due to an inadequate economic policy, the US dollar devalued by a coefficient of 68.16. Eight of the former US presidents, starting in 1961, were not fully aware of this fact. Luckily for the US, in 2017 a person became president who looks at the problem of external debt with competence and from whom one can expect to have the concept of how to solve this problem.

Over a period of six years (2005 to 2010), the average annual growth rate of the gross domestic product of the US was 0.48 percent. During this same period, the growth rate of foreign debt was 9.82 percent. It follows that the country's external debt grew over twenty times faster. To repay only that part of the external debt, an annual supplementary growth of the gross domestic product of about 1 percent over ten years is required. This can be seen from the precise mathematical calculation in the following two tables.

Table 3: Standard Model of the Upper Limit of the Ability to Repay the External Debt of the State

Maturity: 30 years

Annual interest: 1%

The depreciation coefficient: 0.03874811

The state budget deficit: 0

Size of the state external debt to the size of the gross domestic product of the state (D) in %	Size of the state budget to the gross domestic product of the state (B) in %	Factor of transformation of the external debt of the state into the budget category D (F = x 100) B	Required annual GDP growth of the state to repay external debt of the state (G) in % (F x 0.03874811)
10	38	26.3	1.0
20	38	52.6	2.0
30	38	78.9	3.1

Table 4: Repayment of Government Bonds

Deadline: 100 years

Annual yield: 1%

The depreciation coefficient: 0.0158 6574

The state budget deficit: 0

Size of the state external debt to the size of the gross domestic product of the state (D) in %	Size of the state budget to the gross domestic product of the state (B) in %	Factor of transformation of the external debt of the state into the budget category D (F = x 100) B	Required annual GDP growth of the state to repay external debt of the state(G) in % (F x 0.01586574)
10	38	26.3	0.42
20	38	52.6	0.83
30	38	78.9	1.25
40	38	105.3	1.67
50	38	131.6	2.09
60	38	156.9	2.49
70	38	184.2	2.92
80	38	210.5	3.34
90	38	236.8	3.76
100	38	263.2	4.18

Chapter 4

Historical Dynamics of the External Debt Growth

The economy of the United States accounts for about 24 percent of the world economy today, and the state of that economy is not good. This can be assessed simply by the degree of indebtedness. The total government debt in February 2014 exceeded $17.29 billion, while the gross domestic product was $16.108 billion. Consequently, the national debt is equal to 107 percent of one year's gross domestic product. At the same time, that debt makes up 33 percent of the world's total economic debt. Thus, the indebtedness of the US greatly exceeds the world average. This is the first sign of an oncoming economic collapse.

To better understand this, it is useful to observe the tendencies of development of the US debt. In doing so, the economic policies of individual electoral periods should be evaluated:

1. From 1961 to 1969, during the reign of J. F. Kennedy and L. B. Johnson, the American national debt rose from 297 to 385 billion US dollars, or 29.6% (Democratic Party).
2. From 1969 to 1977, during the reign of R. M. Nixon and G. R. Ford, the national debt increased

      from 385 to 817 billion US dollars, or 112.2% (Republican Party).

3. From 1977 to 1981, during the reign of J. E. Carter, the state's debt rose from 817 to 907 billion US dollars, or 11.0% (Democratic Party).

4. From 1981 to 1989, during the reign of R. W. Reagan, the national debt rose from 907 billion to 2.089 billion US dollars, or 130.3% (Republican Party).

5. From 1989 to 1993, during the reign of G. H. W. Bush, the national debt rose from 2.089 to 3.065 billion US dollars, or 46.7% (Republican Party).

6. From 1993 to 2001, during the reign of W. J. Clinton, the national debt rose from 3.065 to 5.674 billion US dollars, or 85% (Democratic Party).

7. From 2001 to 2009, during the reign of G. W. Bush, the national debt rose from 5.674 to 13.768 billion US dollars, or 142.7% (Republican Party).

8. From 2009 to 2014, during the reign of B. Obama, the state debt rose from 13.768 to 20.245 billion US dollars or 47.0%.

The above data shows how the American political parties managed the economy and how they contributed to the enormous national debt.

Table 5: External Debt of the United Stats

Year	Amount of external debt (in billions of dollars)	Index
1961	297	100
1969	385	130
1977	817	275
1981	907	305
1989	2,089	703
1993	3,065	1,032
2001	5,674	1,910
2009	13,768	4,636
2013	17,200	5,791
2017	20,245	6,816

Table 5 shows that the average annual growth of the external debt of the United States from 1961 to 2013 was 111 percent.

If the budget deficit remains at zero, this part of the debt could be repaid in 100 years with an annual growth of the gross domestic product of 4.36 percent. Based on the data on the average growth of the US GDP over the last 223 years of 3.8 percent, it can be concluded that the necessary growth rate of 4.36 percent cannot be realized, and this debt will enter the category of "eternal debt."

On October 17, 2013, after sixteen days of negotiations, the Republican and the Democratic parties in the United States Congress agreed to raise the level of the government's indebtedness for the 2014 fiscal year. In doing so, they ensured that government departments and institutions would function normally until January 15, 2014. The technical bankruptcy of the state budget was avoided, but it also raised the US debt to the highest level in history. The consequences of the US debt problem were manifested in the slowing of economic growth and the loss of nearly 120,000 jobs.

The American economy is going through its most difficult period in its history. Even people who do not have complete insight into the functioning of multi-economics foresee the need for a new war to create conditions for an economic boom. By doing so, by the logic of economic regularities, the country's economy will begin to recover and grow. While the average economic growth over the past 223 years is 3.8 percent, from 2000–10 it was just 1.9 percent. That is the second worst decade in the country's history. The first such period was from 1790–1800.

The current economic deviation rose from a transfer of part of the country's production into less developed states. This can be successfully repaired by appropriate economic policies.

The American concept of a completely free economy without the need for economic balance carries a devastating virus of economic deviations.

Table 6 shows the annual dynamics of growth of the external debt through election periods. The table shows that the growth of the external debt of the US at the time of Trump's mandate was among the smallest in all presidential elections and the smallest compared with that of the mandates of the Republican presidents. That's a good sign.

Table 6: Dynamics of external debt through presidential periods.

Election Period	President	The Average Annual Growth of Debt (%) (4-3):N:3
1961–1969	J. F. Kennedy and L. B. Johnson	3.7
1969–1977	R. M. Nixon and G. R. Ford	14.0
1977–1981	J. E. Carter	2.8
1981–1989	R. W. Reagan	16.3
1989–1993	G. H. W. Bush	11.7
1993–2001	W. J. Clinton	10.6
2001–2009	G. W. Bush	17.8
2009–2017	B. Obama	5.9
2017–2019	D. Trump	2.7

Chapter 5

The Problem of Imbalances in Exports and Imports

The economy of the US has the need and the interest to introduce foreign trade into its structure. The basic principle of that trade is its value balance. The value of imports should be covered by the value of exports. However, all data from practice shows that this equality is rarely established. One of the states always has a higher value of imports than exports. This is the case in the world's most developed countries. This imbalance can be suitably expressed mathematically. When the value of imports of one partner country is mathematically divided by the value of exports to its partner country, an import quotient is obtained. If the quotient has a value greater than one, and if it is repeated in a period greater than one year, then it is an economic deviation. The US quotient is greater than one in relation to some of the world's less developed countries.

With nine major partner states, the US had an import quotient of 1.81. The quotient gradually decreased, and in fell to 1.27 in 2010. This shows a deviation in foreign trade. The solution to this is to establish a balance of exports and imports. This cannot be achieved by forbidding imports or imposing a high rate of duty for some specific countries, because the provisions of free international trade do not allow it. It can be achieved only by market economic means, which means leaving the daily exchange rate of the domestic currency in foreign trade and the introduction of monthly exchange rates of diversified money. Such an approach does not discriminate. It provides equality of the value of imports and exports, thus eliminating economically unjustified damage to one of the partner countries.

The difference between the exchange rates of the two above categories of money is in the formation of the exchange rate. The exchange rate of *ordinary money* is formed on the basis of the relation of supply and demand of foreign currencies to the local currency. The exchange rate of *diversified money* is formed on the basis of the relationship of import and export payments.

The diversified exchange rate is determined for each country separately and is not determined daily but monthly. This exchange rate can only be higher than the general current exchange rate. The daily exchange rate is converted into the diversified one by using the monthly import quotient and the volume of repayments of earlier deficits. Since the diversification exchange rates are issued and published every month, it can be easily and quickly adapted to the current state of economic relations. These exchange rates for individual countries should be established by commercial banks in accordance with the central bank.

Chapter 6

Solving the Problems of
Exports and Imports Imbalance

For a long-term solution of the current problem of imbalance in exports and imports in the United States, an appropriate strategy needs to be created. It must be related to the reduction and repayment of the external debt. It is first necessary to specify exactly what this strategy entails. It is how some available resources are to be used in order to exploit available opportunities to reduce the size of the external debt. In this particular case, it means determining a way for external trading. This is knowledge about the process of applying a diversified money project. This procedure will be described below.

The US has reached a high level of external indebtedness. The total amount of this debt in 2018 amounted to more than 21.040 billion dollars, which is a risk that an economic deviation could be created (collapsing, debacle). The negative consequences of such deviations can be incalculably large. Therefore, this problem should start to be quickly and earnestly solved. The solution to this is to introduce the concept of domestic diversified money according to the further described project.

Project for the Introduction of Diversified Money

(Assuming diversified money is a new variant for settling accounts in foreign trade)

1. The Import Quotient as the Basis for the Introduction of Diversified Money

The US has economic relationships with other countries. A characteristic of these partnerships is such that they are not value-balanced. Data from practice shows that one of these states always has a higher value of imports than exports.

When the value of imports of one partner country is mathematically divided by the value of exports into the partner country, the import quotient is obtained. If the quotient has a value greater than one, and if this is repeated during a period greater than one year, then it is an economic problem.

Table 7: Determination of the Import Quotient for the US in 2005

Mark	Country	Export	Import	Import quotient
01	Canada	211.9	290.4	1.37
02	Mexico	120.4	170.1	1.41
03	Japan	55.5	138.0	2.49
04	China	41.9	243.5	5.81
05	UK	38.6	51.0	1.32
06	Germany	34.2	84.8	2.48
07	South Korea	27.8	43.8	1.58
08	France	22.4	33.8	1.51
09	Taiwan	22.1	34.8	1.58
	Total	**601.3**	**1,090.2**	**1.81**

The optimal import quotient for the US in 2005 is shown in Table 8. This is the situation when imports equal exports,

Table 8: The Optimal Import Quotient for the US in 2005

Mark	Country	Export	Import	Import quotient
01	Canada	290.4	290.4	1.00
02	Mexico	170.1	170.1	1.00
03	Japan	138.0	138.0	1.00
04	China	243.5	243.5	1.00
05	UK	51.0	51.0	1.00
06	Germany	84.8	84.8	1.00
07	South Korea	43.8	43.8	1.00
08	France	33.8	33.8	1.00
09	Taiwan	34.8	34.8	1.00
	Total	**1,090.2**	**1,090.2**	**1.00**

Table 7 shows that the US has an import quotient of 1.81 with nine of its major partner countries. The solution for this economic deviation is to introduce the category of domestic diversified money into the area of foreign trade.

2. The Difference between the Categories of Ordinary and Diversified Money

The difference between the two categories of money is in the formation of the exchange rate.

The exchange rate of *ordinary money* is determined by the supply and demand of the major world currencies against the local currency. The course of the category of *diversified money* is formed on the basis of the relationship of the values of imports and exports.

The general exchange rate is subject to daily fluctuations. These oscillations can be depreciations or appreciations. The diversified course is not a general exchange rate. This is the course of domestic currency that is derived from foreign trade. It is determined for each country separately, and it is not determined daily, but monthly. This course can only be higher than the general exchange rate. The daily exchange rate is converted into the diversified one using the monthly import quotient.

3. Calculation and Determination of the Diversification Courses

The basis for the calculation and determination of diversification courses is the import quotient and assessment of the importance of economic relations with a particular foreign country. Since the diversification courses are adopted and published every month, the diversification exchange rate can be easily and quickly adapted to the current state of economic relations. Diversification courses for individual states should be established by a commercial bank in accordance with the central monetary institution.

If, as a hypothetical example, the import of a product in the US is taken that has a price according to the overall rate of $100, then the price of that product by the application of the diversified exchange rate would increase as shown in the Table 9.

Table 9: Hypothetical Example of the Increase of Prices of Imported Products in the US

Imports from the country	The price of imported products by applying the general course	Import quotient	The price of imported products by applying the diversification course
Canada	100	1.37	137
Mexico	100	1.41	141
Japan	100	2.49	249
China	100	5.81	581
UK	100	1.32	132
Germany	100	2.48	248
South Korea	100	1.58	158
France	100	1.51	151
Taiwan	100	1.58	158

Source: Internet.

4. Opening Diversification Bank Accounts

Diversification bank accounts are opened by legal and natural persons engaged in exports or imports. Separate accounts for each foreign country are opened with commercial banks. Diversification accounts have a depository relationship with the bank, and the operations are always done in the local currency.

5. Payment of Exports

After the conclusion of the export agreements, the foreign buyer opens a letter of credit with the commercial bank of the exporter. The letter of credit is opened in favor of the diversification account of the domestic exporter to the agreed value of exports. The received monetary payment has the category of domestic diversified money (for example: 1,000 diversified dollars for Canada).

6. Conversion of Payments from Exports

Upon payment of the agreed amount by the foreign buyer in favor of the diversification account of the exporter, the exporter obtains, for example, US dollars for Canada, Mexico, China, etc. The commercial bank converts this diversified domestic currency at the purchasing diversified exchange rate into normal domestic money. The amount of the normal domestic money is always, according to this calculation, higher than the amount of the domestic diversified money.

7. Purchase of Domestic Diversified Money

The diversified money that the exporter buys from the commercial bank is according to the purchasing diversified course. Thus, the exporter, for example, gets 120 normal dollars for 100 diversified dollars. In this way, he is stimulating exports.

8. Sale of Diversified Money Realized from Exports

After the conclusion of import agreements, or getting the estimate for imports from a foreign country, the importer gives the order to his commercial bank to sell him the required amount of domestic diversified money for that country. If a commercial bank has US dollars on its diversified account for this foreign country, then it issues to the importer the calculation for the sale of the diversified amount of dollars according the selling diversified course. For example: for the import value from country X amounting to 100 dollars, the importer has to pay the diversified equivalent of 122 dollars.

Such a procedure ensures that importers from any foreign country can use only as much money as exporters have created.

9. Publishing the Diversified Courses

Diversified courses are determined and published on the basis of the import quotient for the previous month for each country. These are buying and selling courses.

10. Freedom of Interstate Commerce

The diversified exchange rate affects the volume of interstate commerce of a country with any other country. In fact, there is no trade discrimination against any country. This instrument only produces a balanced state in interstate commerce. Its only purpose is the elimination of economic deviations in trade.

11. The Behavior of Exporters in Terms of the Application of Diversified Money

When the principle of diversified money in interstate commerce is introduced, each exporter behaves economically rational. He directs his exports to that country for which the highest import quotient is published, if other conditions do not prevent such a strategy.

Thus, the exporter will achieve the best financial results, and the deficit of the exporter country will decrease fastest with the countries with which it has the greatest deficit. When exports and imports of the partner countries are balanced, then the import quotient is one and the diversification course becomes equal with the general exchange rate. When this is achieved with all countries, then the economic deviation generated from the imbalance of imports and exports will be completely eliminated.

12. Behavior of the Importers in Terms of the Application of Diversified Money

The behavior of importers will be opposite to that of the exporters. They will normally direct their imports to the country where the smallest import quotient was published, if all other conditions allow such a choice.

13. Effects of the Application of Diversified Money

Diversification courses will have various economic impacts. They will be positive and negative, and will apply to exporters, importers, states, and citizens.

The effects for exporters
The effects for exporters are positive. For them, applying diversified money increases export prices and revenues, as long as the import quotients for the country to which they export are greater than one. When the quotient becomes one, the positive effects cease.

The effects for importers
The effects for importers are not positive. For them, the import prices and expenses increase as long as the import quotients for the state from which they import are greater than one. When they become one, the negative effects cease.

Effects for the state
The positive effects for the state of the external debtor will be generated in several ways:

- New current account deficits are eliminated
- Foreign countries are forced to cover their exports by imports
- The volume of production and employment is increased
- The gross domestic product and tax revenues are increased
- The country's interest costs are decreased
- The country's exporting firms become more profitable

- The economic fruits, earnings, and purchasing power in the country are increased
- The economic power of the country becomes stronger

Effects for citizens

The effects for the citizens after the introduction of domestic diversified money are partly unfavorable because imported goods and services become more expensive. On the other side, they are positive, because they increase the possibility of domestic production and employment of a part of the unemployed population.

14. Limitation of Resources

Since importers from individual countries can pay only with diversified money for these countries, it is a limited economic resource that is subject to monthly fluctuations.

15. Control of Imports

The native or legal immigrant who imports goods from abroad will need to attach a customs document on the payment of the goods out of the diversified bank account.

16. Conclusions

Based on the analysis of the concept of domestic diversified money, several conclusions can be drawn:

1. The diversification temporarily depreciates domestic currency for each foreign country in different intensities, depending on the size of the imbalance of imports and exports.
2. The purpose of the depreciation is a temporary increase in the price of imports from an individual

foreign country and the support of exports to that country.

3. The task of the temporary depreciation is the balance of exports and imports.

4. The level of depreciation depends on the size of the imbalance of imports and exports: a greater imbalance brings a higher level of depreciation, and a small imbalance a lesser one.

5. The depreciation is defined so that the fastest balance of imports and exports is achieved with those countries where the imbalance is the greatest.

6. When the balance of exports and imports is established, the diversification regime ends.

7. The regime of diversified domestic money economically forces the partner countries to eliminate the economic deviations resulting from the imbalance of imports and exports.

17. Possible Usefulness of Introducing Diversified Money

On August 4, 2014, the US external debt amounted to 17.606 billion dollars. Compared with 2013, it increased by about 820 billion, or about 4.9 percent. A year earlier, it increased by about 610 billion dollars, or about 3.7 percent. Its increase is absolute and relative.

The growth of the external debt shows that the state is in the process of collapsing. If this growth is not stopped quickly and efficiently, its tendency will continue progressively, and its continuation can quickly result in a state of economic debacle, with dire unforeseeable consequences. The debt is now so large that it cannot be restored from the state budget in a hundred years. This is the result of the deficit in foreign trade. This is a big problem for both the internal and external security of the US. This problem can be solved by the state introducing the category of diversified money into foreign trade transactions.

Solving this problem can be carried out in three phases: The first is to eliminate the annual payment deficit in foreign trade; the second phase, which follows immediately and in parallel with the first, the domestic production, and thus the gross domestic product, is increased by the substitution of imports; in the third phase, the decrease of the total debt starts from secondary sources and effects.

The calculation looks like this:

1. The current annual export value can be increased by 820 billion dollars, while the imports may stay the same or decrease. Thus, the current annual foreign trade deficit as a whole is eliminated.
2. From the increased state revenues, based on the growth of production and gross domestic product from the annual import substitution, a further increase in the value of exports can be stimulated, to the value of about 300 billion dollars a year.
3. The annual export of nonmaterial products, energy, and tourism can reduce the total debt by about 450 billion dollars.

Such a structure can achieve two effects: The first is that the annual exports and imports are balanced; the second is that the total current annual debt could be reduced by about 750 billion dollars, resulting in the possibility of eliminating it entirely in about twenty-four years.

Internal diversified money is a useful tool that can bring great economic benefits to the US, as well as for all other developed states of the world. These benefits during the next twenty years could amount to more than 50 trillion dollars.

Today, in the US and worldwide, the imminent apocalyptic slogan "Coming Economic Collapse" is spread, predicting the consequences of what happened in 1929. But it was a primarily economic deviation for the US, a surplus of production, and the one that is to come would be a secondary one, a deficit of production. There are two possibilities of what could come. The first is negative and leads to a level of national disaster; the second is positive and encouraging and leads to the solution of the problem of external debt.

If the first dangerous one happens, the US will lose its economic leadership in the world, entering a phase of gradual impoverishment, and becoming a prisoner of its external debts. Somewhat earlier than in the US, something similar could start to happen in the United Kingdom, France, Italy, Japan, and Germany. In the end, it also would severely hit China, India, Russia, and Brazil. Then the situation in world economics could no longer be controlled. There would be economic disaster and chaos on a large scale.

If the positive option happens, the US could generate an annual financial benefit of about 1.57 trillion. Such success would then be carried over to the world, causing positive changes, and the US would preserve its authority as the first economic power of the world.

Economic collapse

As a start of an economic collapse, a conceptual fact of exceeding two border economic parameters will be taken: The repayment of foreign debt within the working period of one human generation of thirty years, and an annual interest rate on the debt of 1 percent. These two parameters are the upper limit of the conditions in which a country can borrow.

In Table 11, based on these two parameters, the minimum amount of the annual increase of the gross domestic product from which it is possible to repay such a debt of the state will be calculated. A state that cannot fit into the framework of these two parameters is economically collapsing.

The US has an external debt of 102.7 percent of the GDP and does not generate a mathematically equivalent GDP growth that allows for the repayment of such a debt. It can be considered an economically collapsing state.

Table 10: Standard Model of the Ability to Repay the External Debt of the State

Maturity: 30 years

Annual interest: 1%

The depreciation coefficient: 0.03874811

The state budget deficit: 0

Size of the external debt of the state in relation to the size of the gross domestic product of the state in %	Size of the state budget in relation to the size of the gross domestic product of the state in %	Factor of transformation of the external debt of the state into the budget category	Required annual GDP growth to repay the external debt of the state in %
10	38	26.3	1.0
20	38	52.6	2.0
30	38	78.9	3.1

Table 11: The Economic Collapsing of the US from 2005–2012

Year	Size of the external debt of the state in relation to the size of the gross domestic product	Annual growth of the gross domestic product	Maximum size of the external debt in relation to the size of the gross domestic product	Minimum annual growth of gross domestic product for the repayment of the external debt of the state	Deviation of the size of the external debt (2:4)	Deviation of the GDP growth (3:5)
1	2	3	4	5	6	7
2005	60	3.4	30	3.1	2.00	1.10
2006	61	2.7	30	3.1	2.03	0.87
2007	62	1.8	30	3.1	2.07	0.58
2008	68	-0.3	30	3.1	2.27	- 0.10
2009	83	-2.8	30	3.1	2.77	-5.90
2010	90	2.5	30	3.1	3.00	0.81
2011	95	1.8	30	3.1	3.17	0.58
2012	98	2.8	30	3.1	3.27	0.90
Standard	30	3.1		3.1	1.00	1.00

The data in Table 11 shows that the US was in a state of economic collapse according to the two economic criteria: the largest foreign debt in eight years and the rate of growth of the gross domestic product for seven years. External debt has exceeded the upper limit of the allowed debt by 2.27 times, or 68 percent of the gross domestic product. Column six of the table shows that this overdraft had a tendency of continuous growth. In 2005, it already had a level of 2.00, and by 2012 it had increased to the level of 3.27. At the same time, a minimum GDP growth was reached only in 2005. In all subsequent years, this growth was not achievable. This can be seen in column seven of the table. The collapse constantly intensified from 2005 to 2012.

The external debt of the US grew at the expense of reducing the volume of domestic production. This was the result of an insufficiently regulated model of free trade and the lack of a corresponding reaction in the concept of the economic policy.

To realize the planned project of domestic diversified money in the US, a special law should be issued on domestic diversified money for use in foreign trade, and then financial regulations and procedures at the level of the central monetary authority, the Fed, should be enacted.

Chapter 7

The Organic Connection of Production and Consumption in the State

Production and consumption are closely connected by revenue. The volume of consumption is generated from production revenues. This is an economic principle. It is not possible to spend something that is not produced, nor is it possible to spend more than is produced. For example: it is not possible for one liter of water to fill a container of two liters. From this follows the conclusion that there must be an equality of production and consumption. This is generally shown in Scheme 1.

Scheme 1: Structure of the Value of Production and Consumption

Production	Consumption
Manufacture of basic materials Production of various auxiliary materials Production of electricity Production of energy (oil, gas) Production of various services	Consumption of basic materials Consumption of various auxiliary materials Electricity consumption Consumption of energy (oil, gas) Consumption of various services

Production	Consumption
Saving for the replacement of fixed assets	Consumption of fixed assets
The service rents	Consumption of services rent
The work of employees	Consumption of services by employees
Services for pensions and health	Consumption arising from pensions and health
Government services	Consumption of state services
Credit services	Consumption of credit services
Total	**Total**

This equality of values is derived from the principle of economic duals as an economic law. This principle exists at the micro- and macro-economic levels.

Aggregation of economic micro-duals creates the economic macro-dual or complex product. Aggregation can be performed according to three possible criteria: addition by space, addition by time, and addition by type. The macro-dual has all the elements that its micro-duals have. It also is in economic balance. In it are the aggregate elements that make the balance between production and consumption. This is illustrated in Scheme 2.

Scheme 2: The Economic Macro-dual

Aggregates of values of offer – production	Aggregates of values of demand – consumption
Production costs:	Payments received for deliveries of:
*Basic materials	*Basic materials
*Auxiliary materials	*Auxiliary materials
*Electricity	*Electricity
*Energy	*Energy
*Various services	*Various services

Aggregates of values of offer – production	Aggregates of values of demand – consumption
*Depreciation *Rent *Wages *Contributions *Taxes *Interest	*Depreciation *Rent *Wages *Contributions *Taxes *Interest
Total value of production	**Total value of consumption**

This form of economic balance of production and consumption is optimal. It is generally supplemented by size of exports and imports. This is illustrated in Scheme 3.

Scheme 3: Economic Macro-dual with a Positive Balance

Aggregates of values of production and import	Aggregates of values of consumption and Export
Production costs: basic materials various auxiliary materials electricity energy various services depreciation rent wages contributions taxes interest	Payments received for: - basic materials - auxiliary materials - electricity - energy - various services - depreciation - rent - wages - contributions - taxes - interest
Total value	Total value
Costs of imports Revenue for exports	Payments for imports Received payments for exports
Total	**Total**

Such a model can be deviant if the cost of imports remains uncovered by exports. Such a generated deviation is complex. Its effects to the economy of the state are insolvency and inflation. Such a model is shown in Scheme 4.

Scheme 4: Economic Macro-dual with a Negative Balance

Aggregates of values of production and imports	Aggregates of values of consumption and exports
Production costs: basic materials auxiliary materials electricity energy various services depreciation rent wages contributions taxes interest	Payments received for: - basic materials - auxiliary materials - electricity - energy - various services - depreciation - rent - wages - contributions - taxes - interest
Total value	Total value
Costs of imports Revenues for exports	Payments for imports Received payments for exports
Uncovered costs of imports by exports (loss)	Foreign debts (decrease of the property of the state)
Total	**Total**

The principle of equality of production and consumption is the fundamental principle of the economic policy of the state. By this principle, economic stability is established. By moving away from this principle, economic stability collapses and an economic deviation is produced. The equality and balance of production and consumption creates three beneficial effects:

1. The application of this principle creates stability in the state's economy, which is especially important in various crisis economic situations when impacts to this stability are generated. This can be world political deviations, earthquakes, floods, political instability in the country, and great climate changes.

2. By the application of this principle, the state avoids entering into the economic deviation of debt relations to foreign countries due to consumption based on imports. This debt relation causes a reduction in future spending because of servicing credit debt, increasing interest costs, and limiting future economic development.

3. A full application of this principle maintains the optimum economic power of the state and all derivatives of this power. These include national defense, external political reputation, internal political stability, progress in education, health, social protection, and research of various types and levels.

Chapter 8

The Balance of Exports and Imports
and Diversified Money

Exporters and Importers Under Conditions of the Application of Diversified Money

When introducing the category of diversified money into interstate commerce, every exporter behaves economically rational. He directs his exports to that country for which the highest import quotient has been published, if other conditions do not prevent such an orientation. Thus, the exporter will achieve the best financial results, and the deficit of the exporter state will decline fastest in the countries with which there is currently the largest deficit. When the exports and imports of the partner states are balanced, the import quotient is one and the diversification exchange rate becomes equal with the general exchange rate of the currency. When this is achieved with all countries, the economic deviation generated from an imbalance of exports and imports of the state will be completely eliminated.

The behavior of importers will be the opposite of exporters. They will direct their imports toward the country where the smallest import quotient was published, normally if all other conditions allow such a choice.

Diversification exchange rates will have more economic effects, which will be positive and negative and apply to exporters, importers, the state, and citizens.

The effects on exporters are positive. By applying diversified money, their export prices and revenues increase as long as the import quotients for the country to which they export are greater than one. When this quotient becomes one, the positive effects come to an end.

The effects of importers are not positive. Their import prices and expenses increase as long as the import quotients for the state from which they import are greater than one. When they become one, the negative effects stop.

The positive effects for the state of the external debtor will be generated in several ways:

- New current account deficits are eliminated
- Foreign states are forced to cover their exports to some states by the imports
- The volume of production and employment in the debtor countries is increased
- The gross domestic product and tax revenues of the debtor country are increased
- For the state of the debtor, the costs of interest on debt are reduced
- The exporting firms of the debtor country become more profitable
- The economic fruits, earnings, and purchasing power in the country of the debtor are increased
- The economic power of the debtor state strengthens.

The effects for the citizens, after introducing the domestic diversified money, are partly unfavorable, because imported goods and services become more expensive. On the other side they are positive, because the possibility of domestic production and employment of a part of unemployed citizens is increased.

The Establishment of Equality of Exports and Imports

The purpose of the temporary appreciation of the domestic currency at import is its rise in prices from some individual foreign country and a support of export to that given country. Thus, exports and imports become balanced. By the regime of diversified domestic currency, the partner countries are forced to eliminate the economic deviations resulting from an imbalance of imports and exports.

Solving the problem of inequality of exports and imports can be in three phases: In the first phase, the annual payment deficit in foreign trade is eliminated; in the second, which follows immediately and in parallel with the first, the substitution of imports increases the domestic production and thus the gross domestic product; during the third phase, the total debt from secondary sources and effects starts to decrease.

As an example of external indebtedness, 50 world countries will be used to show in this example the danger of economic debacle. States that have large external debts will not be able to return this debt within a hundred years. In addition, they will have the big problem of the interruption of successive going into debt. This can be seen in table 10.

Criteria for evaluating the risk of economic debacle are determined so that the amount of foreign debt relative to the size of the GDP includes an appropriate degree of danger.

Table 12: The degree of risk of foreign debts

Category	Height of external debt relative to the size of GDP	The degree of risk
A	0.001 – 0.299	No
B	0.300 – 0.399	Very small
C	0.400 – 0.499	Small
D	0.500 – 0.999	Medium
E	1.000 – 1.999	Large
F	2.000 and more	Very large

Table 13: Risk of Economic Debacle

State	External debt (Millions of US \$)	Domestic gross product (Millions of US \$)	External debt to GDP (2:3)	The limit for the amount of external debt to GDP	Height of external Over-indebted-ness (4-5)	The risk of economic debacle
USA	14,456,194	14,582,400	0.991	0.300	0.691	Medium
UK	9,554,857	2,246,079	4.254	0.300	3.954	Very large
Germany	5,217,014	3,309,669	1.576	0.300	1.276	Large
France	5,091,260	2,560,002	1.989	0.300	1.689	Large
Japan	2,588,607	5,497,813	0.471	0.300	0.171	Small
Italy	2,435,220	2,051,412	1.187	0.300	0.887	Large
Netherlands	2,433,884	783,413	3.107	0.300	2.807	Very large
Spain	2,316,691	1,407,405	1.646	0.300	1.346	Large
Ireland	2,303,419	203,892	11.297	0.300	10.997	Very large
Luxembourg	1,915,942	55,096	34.775	0.300	34.475	Very large
Belgium	1,292,068	467,472	2.764	0.300	2.464	Very large
Switzerland	1,287,359	523,772	2.458	0.300	2.158	Very large
Australia	1,167,884	924,843	1.263	0.300	0.963	Large
Canada	1,106,998	1,574,052	0.703	0.300	0.403	Medium

State	External debt (Millions of US $)	Domestic gross product (Millions of US $)	External debt to GDP (2:3)	The limit for the amount of external debt to GDP	Height of external Over-indebted-ness (4-5)	The risk of economic debacle
Sweden	945,086	458,004	2.063	0.300	1.763	Very large
Hong Kong	803,416	224,458	3.579	0.300	3.279	Very large
Austria	797,790	376,162	2.121	0.300	1.821	Very large
Denmark	596,199	310,405	1.921	0.300	1.621	Large
Norway	583,684	414,462	1.408	0.300	1.108	Large
China	548,938	5,878,629	0.093	0.300	0.000	No
Greece	546,607	304,865	1.793	0.300	1.493	Large
Portugal	528,597	228,538	2.313	0.300	2.013	Very large
Russia	489,043	1,479,819	0.330	0.300	0.030	Very small
Finland	441,369	238,801	1.848	0.300	1.548	Large
South Korea	359,985	1,014,483	0.355	0.300	0.055	Very small
Brazil	351,941	2,087,890	0.169	0.300	0.000	No
India	295,891	1,729,010	0.171	0.300	0.000	No
Turkey	289,387	735,264	0.394	0.300	0.094	Very small
Poland	264,574	468,585	0.565	0.300	0.265	Medium

State	External debt (Millions of US $)	Domestic gross product (Millions of US $)	External debt to GDP (2:3)	The limit for the amount of external debt to GDP	Height of external Over-indebtedness (4-5)	The risk of economic debacle
Mexico	250,956	1,039,662	0.241	0.300	0.000	No
Hungary	209,540	130,419	1.607	0.300	1.307	Large
Indonesia	200,050	706,558	0.283	0.300	0.000	No
Argentina	128,600	368,712	0.349	0.300	0.049	Very small
Romania	122,994	161,624	0.761	0.300	0.461	Medium
U. A. Emirates	122,700	230,252	0.533	0.300	0.233	Medium
Iceland	119,435	13,640	8.756	0.300	8.456	Very large
Kazakhstan	119,242	142,987	0.834	0.300	0.534	Medium
Ukraine	117,346	137,929	0.851	0.300	0.551	Medium
Israel	106,018	217,334	0.488	0.300	0.188	Small
Cyprus	103,585	25,039	4.137	0.300	3.837	Very large
Thailand	100,561	318,847	0.315	0.300	0.015	Very small
South Africa	99,005	375,766	0.263	0.300	0.000	No
Czech Republic	95,396	192,152	0.496	0.300	0.196	Small

State	External debt (Millions of US $)	Domestic gross product (Millions of US $)	External debt to GDP (2:3)	The limit for the amount of external debt to GDP	Height of external Over-indebted-ness (4-5)	The risk of economic debacle
Taiwan	91,410	15,936	5.736	0.300	5.436	Very large
Chile	86,738	203,443	0.426	0.300	0.126	Small
Saudi Arabia	82,920	375,766	0.221	0.300	0.000	No
Malaysia	82,171	237,804	0.346	0.300	0.046	Very small
Qatar	71,380	98,313	0.726	0.300	0.426	Medium
Slovakia	66,439	89,034	0.746	0.300	0.446	Medium
Columbia	64,723	288,189	0.225	0.300	0.000	No

Source: Wikipedia

Chapter 9

Rationalization of Foreign Debts

The external debt of the US has steadily grown from 1961 to 2017 at an average annual rate of 9.6 percent. Imports of goods and services in the United States as a percentage of GDP grew 10.53 percent in 1990, 14.32 percent in 2000, and 15.39 percent in 2015. This can be considered a major economic deviation. Foreign states were unilaterally and freely using the US economic space and its purchasing power to sell their products, and by doing also boosted their development. The primary country to do so was the People's Republic of China. Thus, China and other countries created the US external debt. The size of this debt has consistently exceeded the one-year value of the US gross domestic product, until it grew to the size of nearly one-third of the world's collective external debts.

All imported goods into the US economic space were for final consumption. Such consumption does not have its own return capacity. Trade of this kind can be considered economically unfair. In this way, the US economic space is financially depleted. The height of its debt has reached a level that is threatening global economic stability. A commercial relationship of this kind should be reduced to a framework of rationality. The way to do this is to introduce diversified money into the foreign trade and financial system of the US. This does not violate the rules of free international trade. It is a strategic method for establishing a financial equilibrium in foreign trade and economic fairness. This method should be introduced into the US economic and financial system.

There are two steps necessary to rationalize the US external debt: stop further debt growth, and repay it.

Table 14: Comparison of Interest Costs

a.   If further growth of the external debt is not stopped
b.   If further growth of external debt is stopped

Repayment basis:
Growing external debt of 9.6% per annum
Initial external debt: $21,000,000,000,000
Time to calculate interest: 10 years
Interest rate: 3%

Year	Growing external debt	Interest (2 x 0.03)	Stopped external debt	Interest (4 x 0.03)	Positive difference (3 - 5 = 6)
1	2	3	4	5	6
2018	21,000,000,000,000	630,000,000,000	21,000,000,000,000	630,000,000,000	0
2019	23,037,000,000,000	691,111,000,000	21,000,000,000,000	630,000,000,000	61,111,000,000
2020	25,248,552,000,000	757,440,000,000	21,000,000,000,000	630,000,000,000	127,440,000,000
2021	27,672,412,990,000	830,160,000,000	21,000,000,000,000	630,000,000,000	200,160,000,000
2022	30,328,964,630,000	909,840,000,000	21,000,000,000,000	630,000,000,000	279,840,000,000
2023	33,240,545,230,000	997,200,000,000	21,000,000,000,000	630,000,000,000	367,200,000,000
2024	36,431,637,570,000	1,092,930,000,000	21,000,000,000,000	630,000,000,000	462,930,000,000
2025	39,929,074,770,000	1,197,870,000,000	21,000,000,000,000	630,000,000,000	567,870,000,000
2026	43,762,265,940,000	1,312,860,000,000	21,000,000,000,000	630,000,000,000	682,860,000,000
2027	47,963,443,470,000	1,438,890,000,000	21,000,000,000,000	630,000,000,000	808,890,000,000
2028	52,567,934,040,000	1,577,010,000,000	21,000,000,000,000	630,000,000,000	947,010,000,000
Total		11,435,311,000,000		6,930,000,000,000	4,505,311,000,000

The cost savings in this variant for 10 years is $4,505,311,000,000.

Table 15: Comparison of Interest Costs

a.   If further growth of external debt is not stopped
b.   If further growth of external debt is stopped and repaid

Repayment basis
Growing external debt of 9.6% per annum
Initial external debt: $21,000,000,000,000
Time to calculate interest: 10 years
Interest rate: 3%

Year	Growth of external debt	Interest (2 x 0.03)	External debt is stopped and repaid	Interest (4 x 0.03)	Positive difference (3 – 5 = 6)
1	2	3	4	5	6
2018	21,000,000,000,000	630,000,000,000	20,000,000,000,000	630,000,000,000	0
2019	23,037,000,000,000	691,111,000,000	19,000,000,000,000	600,000,000,000	91,111,000,000
2020	25,248,552,000,000	757,440,000,000	18,000,000,000,000	570,000,000,000	187,440,000,000
2021	27,672,412,990,000	830,160,000,000	17,000,000,000,000	540,000,000,000	290,160,000,000
2022	30,328,964,630,000	909,840,000,000	16,000,000,000,000	510,000,000,000	399,840,000,000
2023	33,240,545,230,000	997,200,000,000	15,000,000,000,000	480,000,000,000	517,200,000,000
2024	36,431,637,570,000	1,092,930,000,000	14,000,000,000,000	450,000,000,000	642,930,000,000
2025	39,929,074,770,000	1,197,870,000,000	13,000,000,000,000	420,000,000,000	777,870,000,000
2026	43,762,265,940,000	1,312,860,000,000	12,000,000,000,000	390,000,000,000	922,860,000,000
2027	47,963,443,470,000	1,438,890,000,000	11,000,000,000,000	360,000,000,000	1,078,890,000,000
2028	52,567,931,000,000	1,577,010,000,000	10,000,000,000,000	330,000,000,000	1,247,010,000,000
Total		11,424,311,000,000		5,280,000,000,000	6,144,311,000,000

The cost savings in this variant for 10 years is $6,144,311,000,000

Chapter 10

External Debt of the
United States Should Disappear

The commercial and financial aspects the United States are absolutely important, as it holds a quarter of the world's economic power. Despite that, it is also the largest external debtor in the world. It's a heavy stone for the US. In view of such a debt, the US cannot fully realize its role in the world.

The external debt of the US has been building for decades and cannot disappear overnight. This process will take a long time, but the US cannot even begin to start that process if no organization is created. That organization includes the method of treatment and resources that will be used for that purpose. The category of diversified money in foreign trade is one method for such a task. Positive effects, in the form of financial gain and resources, are obtained by applying this method.

The external debt of the US, according to estimates, will grow to \$52,567,934,040,000 in the next ten years if nothing is changed in US economic policy. With this increase, that debt could cause economic catastrophe for the US and all countries that are strongly connected to its economic system. This increase is shown in Table 16.

Table 16: Predictable annual growth in external debt and interest costs

Year	Annual growth of external debt 9.6%	Interest 3%
2018	21,000,000,000,000	630,000,000,000
2019	23,037,000,000,000	691,111,000,000
2020	25,248,552,000,000	757,440,000,000
2021	27,672,412,990,000	830,160,000,000
2022	30,328,964,630,000	909,840,000,000
2023	33,240,545,230,000	997,200,000,000
2024	36,431,637,570,000	1,092,930,000,000
2025	39,929,074,770,000	1,197,870,000,000
2026	43,762,265,940,000	1,312,860,000,000
2027	47,963,443,470,000	1,438,890,000,000
2028	52,567,934,040,000	1,577,010,000,000
Total		**11,424,311,000,000**

In this paper, it was found that the external debt of the US may be amortized over a period of about ten years and that the effect may be an increase in the annual growth rate of the gross domestic product up to 5 percent.

If no external debt rationalization is undertaken, it will grow at a predictable average rate of 9.6 percent. The same dynamics also apply to the growth of interest.

Chapter 11

Economic Benefits from the
Introduction of Diversified Money

The research carried out by this work has shown that the benefits of rationalizing the external debt of the state through diversified money can be multiple and very large. The scenario involves reducing the external debt of the US to:

- stop the growth of the entire debt
- repay half of the debt
- do this over a period of ten years

The financial effects of this scenario are shown in Table 17.

Table 17
Initial external debt: $21,000,000,000,000
Time to calculate interest: 10 years
Interest rate: 3%

Year	Growth of external debt	Interest (2 x 0.03)	External debt is stopped and repaid	Interest (4 x 0.03)	Positive difference (3 - 5 = 6)
1	2	3	4	5	6
2018	21,000,000,000,000	630,000,000,000	20,000,000,000,000	630,000,000,000	0
2019	23,037,000,000,000	691,111,000,000	19,000,000,000,000	600,000,000,000	91,111,000,000
2020	25,248,552,000,000	757,440,000,000	18,000,000,000,000	570,000,000,000	187,440,000,000
2021	27,672,412,990,000	830,160,000,000	17,000,000,000,000	540,000,000,000	290,160,000,000
2022	30,328,964,630,000	909,840,000,000	16,000,000,000,000	510,000,000,000	399,840,000,000
2023	33,240,545,230,000	997,200,000,000	15,000,000,000,000	480,000,000,000	517,200,000,000
2024	36,431,637,570,000	1,092,930,000,000	14,000,000,000,000	450,000,000,000	642,930,000,000
2025	39,929,074,770,000	1,197,870,000,000	13,000,000,000,000	420,000,000,000	777,870,000,000
2026	43,762,265,940,000	1,312,860,000,000	12,000,000,000,000	390,000,000,000	922,860,000,000
2027	47,963,443,470,000	1,438,890,000,000	11,000,000,000,000	360,000,000,000	1,078,890,000,000
2028	52,567,931,000,000	1,577,010,000,000	10,000,000,000,000	330,000,000,000	1,247,010,000,000
Total		11,424,311,000,000		5,280,000,000,000	6,144,311,000,000

Table 18: Financial benefit from using diversified money

Year	Financial benefit of using diversified money for a 10-year period	Financial benefit from eliminating the growth of interest expenses	Annual growth of the GDP from eliminating the growth of import	Total financial benefit (2+3+4) = 5
1	2	3	4	5
2018	0	0	0	0
2019	2,037,000,000,000	91,111,000,000	1,008,500,000,000	3,136,611,000,000
2020	2,211,552,000,000	187,440,000,000	1,105,776,000,000	3,504,768,000,000
2021	2,423,860,000,000	290,160,000,000	1,121,930,000,000	3,835,950,000,000
2022	2,656,552,000,000	399,840,000,000	1,328,276,000,000	4,384,668,000,000
2023	2,911,581,000,000	517,200,000,000	1,455,791,000,000	4,884,572,000,000
2024	3,191,091,000,000	641,930,000,000	1,595,546,000,000	5,428,567,000,000
2025	3,497,437,000,000	777,870,000,000	1,748,719,000,000	6,024,026,000,000
2026	3,833,190,000,000	992,890,000,000	1,916,595,000,000	6,742,675,000,000
2027	4,201,178,000,000	1,078,890,000,000	2,100,589,000,000	7,380,657,000,000
2028	4,604,490,000,000	1,247,010,000,000	2,302,245,000,000	8,153,745,000,000
Total	31,567,931,000,000	6,224,341,000,000	15,684,063,000,000	53,476,335,000,000

Thereafter, an unpaid remainder of the external debt of $10,000,000,000,000 can be repaid in one payment from accumulated financial gains from 2018 to 2028.

Financial benefits for the United States from using the category of diversified money during a 10-year period are:

If growth of external debt is stopped and reduced:
$31,567,931,000,000

Interest expenses if growth of external debt is stopped:
$6,224,341,000,000

Growth of the GDP if growth of external debt is stopped:
$15,684,063,000,000

Total:	**$53,476,335,000,000**
Unpaid external debt:	$10,000,000,000,000
Net benefit:	**$43,476,335,000,000**

In addition to the above-mentioned economic savings, there is also a rise in the degree of economic security. The current quotient of economic security rises from current 0.49 to 1.00.

The method of diversified money in foreign trade optimizes foreign-trade operations at the state level. This fulfills four criteria for the economic optimum:

- Accuracy of the state economic data
- Good intentions of state economic policy
- Objective limitations in the state's economy
- The best economic result

Chapter 12

Conclusions

Based on the foregoing research and findings, it is possible to draw important conclusions about the United States economy. These conclusions are important because, on that basis, state bodies could and should check the current functions in the field of foreign trade.

These conclusions are unlikely to be pleasant for the United States. It will be necessary to check whether the current economic policy works on the principle of "spoiled fingernail," meaning that the nail starts to spoil from the top. It begins to lose a healthy light-pink color and gradually takes on a sick and unpleasant rotten, yellowish color.

We can draw the following conclusions from this work:

1. The United States has a very big economic problem in the form of a large and threatening foreign debt, a debt this country should not have because it is large and naturally rich with many exceptional people. These properties make it capable of resisting any evil. It also has the most important person, the president, who is able and competent to do many good things for his homeland.

2. The former presidents, starting in 1961, did not take sufficient account of the problem of external

debt, so it has grown steadily to today's scary size. This magnitude has grown to about one-third of all external debts in the world, though the share of the United States' gross domestic product accounts for about one-quarter of the world's GDP. From these two facts we can see the existence of the country's over-indebtedness and the existence of a large economic deviation.

3. The economic deviation of the excessively large external debt of the United States can be eliminated, but it is a big and difficult task that can only be solved by applying the economic method of the category of diversified money in foreign trade. For this reason, the United States should redeem the right to use that method for their economic space. The method is the intellectual property of the author of this work. He can be contacted at ovcaricek.ivan@gmail.com.

4. This work should be available to all US partner countries, to ensure that they understand that the economic procedures that should follow are not a violation of the rules of free international trade or an attack on their economic rights, but that it is an objective effort to make United States economics fair, and also to prevent the destruction of the economic power of the United States by partner countries.

5. It is proposed to the president of the United States to initiate proceedings so that the external debt of the United States does not continue to further grow uncontrollably, and the economy to become sluggish, causing its repayment ability to begin to decrease.

External Debt of States in the World.

Data sources

List of countries by external debt

Rank	Country/Region	External debt US dollars	Date	Per capita US dollars	% of GDP
1	United States	1.9765887×10^{13}	31 December 2018 [1]	58,200	115
2	United Kingdom	8.475956×10^{12}	31 December 2017 [2]	127,000	313
3	France	5.689745×10^{12}	31 December 2017 [3]	87,200	213
4	Germany	5.398267×10^{12}	31 December 2017 [4]	65,600	141
5	Netherlands	4.5104×10^{12}	31 December 2017 [5]	265,400	522
6	Luxembourg	3.781×10^{12}	31 December 2017 [6]	6,968,000	6,307
7	Japan	3.586817×10^{12}	31 December 2017 [7]	28,200	74
8	Italy	2.51069×10^{12}	31 December 2017 [8]	42,300	124
9	Spain	2.259127×10^{12}	31 December 2017 [9]	48,700	167
10	Canada	1.9319×10^{12}	31 December 2017 [10]	52,300	115
11	China	1.8435×10^{12}	31 March 2018 [11]	1,326	15
12	Switzerland	1.820695×10^{12}	31 December 2017 [12]	213,100	269
13	Australia	1.48772×10^{12}	30 June 2017 [13]	60,800	126

List of countries by external debt					
Rank	Country/Region	External debt US dollars	Date	Per capita US dollars	% of GDP
14	Singapore	1.320567×10^{12}	30 June 2017[14]	231,000	453
15	Belgium	1.278465×10^{12}	30 June 2017[15]	112,000	265
16	Hong Kong	$1.08160806 \times 10^{11}$	30 June 2017[16]	14,820	35
17	Sweden	$9.939396629 \times 10^{11}$	30 June 2017[17]	94,500	177
18	Austria	6.3834×10^{11}	30 June 2017[18]	73,100	167
19	Norway	6.044238×10^{11}	30 June 2017[19]	117,000	169
20	Brazil	5.56418×10^{11}	30 September 2017[20]	3,200	30
21	Russia	5.37458×10^{11}	30 September 2017[21]	3,700	40
22	India	5.29×10^{11}	29 June 2018[22]	380	18
23	Denmark	4.91617×10^{11}	30 June 2017[23]	85,700	163
24	Finland	4.83369×10^{11}	30 June 2017[24]	87,500	196
25	Greece	4.76997×10^{11}	31 December 2017[25]	42,800	228
26	Turkey	4.53207×10^{11}	31 December 2017[26]	5,500	53

List of countries by external debt

Rank	Country/Region	External debt US dollars	Date	Per capita US dollars	% of GDP
27	Portugal	4.47022×10^{11}	30 June 2017[27]	43,300	216
28	Mexico	4.37367×10^{11}	31 December 2017[28]	3,300	38
29	South Korea	4.07341×10^{11}	30 June 2017[29]	7,500	27
30	Poland	3.63658×10^{11}	30 June 2017[30]	9,500	70
31	Indonesia	3.35289×10^{11}	30 June 2017[31]	1,300	34
32	Malaysia	2.278445×10^{11}	31 March 2018[32]	6,800	75
33	Ireland	2.276×10^{11}	31 December 2017[33]	49,000	64
34	United Arab Emirates	2.204×10^{11}	31 December 2016 est. [34]	23,500	59
35	Saudi Arabia	2.009×10^{11}	31 December 2016 est. [35]	6,100	31
36	Argentina	3.63117×10^{11}	31 December 2017[36]	8,280	66
37	Mauritius	1.9971×10^{11}	30 June 2018[37]	148,000	1,536
38	Taiwan	1.99051×10^{11}	30 June 2018[38]	7,400	33

List of countries by external debt					
Rank	Country/Region	External debt US dollars	Date	Per capita US dollars	% of GDP
39	New Zealand	1.98815×10^{11}	31 March 2018[39]	40,300	100
40	Chile	1.832943×10^{11}	31 May 2018[40]	9,000	66
—	Puerto Rico	1.674×10^{11}	31 January 2015 est.	47,800	164
41	Kazakhstan	1.65501×10^{11}	31 March 2017[41]	9,100	117
42	Qatar	1.592×10^{11}	31 December 2016 est. [42]	68,100	102
43	Thailand	1.4942955×10^{11}	31 December 2017[43]	2,170	33
44	Hungary	1.48024×10^{11}	30 June 2017[44]	15,000	121
45	South Africa	1.42833×10^{11}	31 December 2016[45]	2,600	48
46	Czech Republic	1.37606×10^{11}	31 December 2016[46]	13,000	70
47	Colombia	1.210972×10^{11}	31 January 2017[47]	2,500	43
48	Cyprus	1.19672×10^{11}	30 June 2017[48]	97,200	597
49	Ukraine	1.14836×10^{11}	30 June 2017[49]	2,600	122
50	Venezuela	1.10878×10^{11}	30 September 2015[50]	3,500	23

List of countries by external debt					
Rank	Country/Region	External debt US dollars	Date	Per capita US dollars	% of GDP
51	Romania	1.0888×10^{11}	31 July 2017[51]	5,100	55
53	Malta	9.62513×10^{10}	30 June 2017[52]	223,000	879
52	Pakistan	1.05841×10^{11}	31 Mar 2019[53]	380	36
54	Israel	8.94384×10^{10}	30 June 2017[54]	10,700	26
55	Slovakia	8.663×10^{10}	30 June 2017[55]	15,900	91
56	Peru	7.46512×10^{10}	31 December 2016[56]	2,300	38
57	Philippines	7.2493×10^{10}	30 June 2017[57]	720	25
58	Iraq	6.801×10^{10}	31 December 2016 est. [58]	1,800	44
59	Egypt	6.73226×10^{10}	31 December 2016[59]	700	41
61	Vietnam	5.09377×10^{10}	31 December 2015[60]	500	26
60	Slovenia	4.995×10^{10}	30 June 2017[61]	24,000	109
61	Morocco	4.88303×10^{10}	30 June 2017[62]	1,400	44

List of countries by external debt					
Rank	Country/Region	External debt US dollars	Date	Per capita US dollars	% of GDP
62	Kuwait	4.789×10^{10}	31 December 2016 est. [63]	11,700	43
63	Sri Lanka	4.65857×10^{10}	31 December 2016[64]	2,200	59
64	Croatia	4.60847×10^{10}	30 June 2017[65]	10,700	87
65	Sudan	4.5×10^{10}	31 December 2015[66]	1,100	47
66	Latvia	4.1147×10^{10}	30 June 2017[67]	21,200	147
67	Bulgaria	4.0419×10^{10}	31 January 2018[68]	5,700	66
68	Belarus	3.8975×10^{10}	30 June 2017[69]	4,000	83
69	Angola	3.77×10^{10}	31 December 2016 est. [70]	1,400	41
70	Ecuador	3.67472×10^{10}	31 August 2017[71]	2,100	35
71	Lithuania	3.64277×10^{10}	30 June 2017[72]	12,700	86
72	Serbia	2.7954×10^{10}	30 June 2017[73]	3,200	78
73	Lebanon	2.7796×10^{10}	31 December 2016[74]	4,600	54

List of countries by external debt

Rank	Country/Region	External debt US dollars	Date	Per capita US dollars	% of GDP
74	Jordan	2.77564×10^{10}	30 June 2017[75]	3,400	30
75	Cuba	2.632×10^{10}	31 December 2016 est. [76]	2,300	34
76	Uruguay	2.61492×10^{10}	31 December 2016[77]	7,600	50
77	Dominican Republic	2.605×10^{10}	31 December 2016 est. [78]	2,400	36
78	Bangladesh	2.5963×10^{10}	30 June 2016[79]	160	12
79	Mongolia	2.5215×10^{10}	30 June 2017[80]	7,800	186
80	Tunisia	2.51247×10^{10}	31 December 2012[81]	2,200	56
81	Costa Rica	2.491×10^{10}	31 December 2016 est. [82]	5,100	43
82	Iceland	2.43906×10^{10}	30 June 2017[83]	72,700	118
83	Ethiopia	2.249×10^{10}	31 December 2016 est. [84]	220	32
84	Kenya	2.21719×10^{10}	30 June 2017[85]	370	26

List of countries by external debt					
Rank	Country/Region	External debt US dollars	Date	Per capita US dollars	% of GDP
85	Papua New Guinea	2.204×10^{10}	31 December 2016 est. [86]	2,800	111
86	Trinidad & Tobago	2.15321×10^{10}	31 December 2016[87]	15,700	76
87	Ghana	2.117×10^{10}	31 December 2016 est. [88]	700	50
88	Bahrain	2.116×10^{10}	31 December 2016 est. [89]	14,900	66
89	Oman	2.085×10^{10}	31 December 2016 est. [90]	4,400	35
90	Estonia	2.05251×10^{10}	31 December 2016[91]	15,700	91
91	Guatemala	1.909×10^{10}	31 December 2016 est. [92]	1,100	28
92	Palau	1.838×10^{10}	31 December 2014 est. [93]	846,000	6,209
93	Panama	1.8341×10^{10}	28 February 2018[94]	4,400	30

List of countries by external debt

Rank	Country/Region	External debt US dollars	Date	Per capita US dollars	% of GDP
94	Bahamas	1.756×10^{10}	31 December 2013 est. [95]	44,200	194
95	Jamaica	1.676×10^{10}	31 December 2016 est. [96]	6,000	122
96	Monaco	1.65×10^{10}	30 June 2010 est.	434,000	240
97	Georgia	1.64165×10^{10}	30 June 2017 [97]	3,900	108
98	Paraguay	1.61224×10^{10}	31 December 2016 [98]	2,400	58
99	Tanzania	1.589×10^{10}	31 December 2016 est. [99]	280	34
100	Uzbekistan	1.575×10^{10}	31 December 2016 est. [100]	500	24
101	Nigeria	1.5047×10^{10}	30 June 2017 [101]	60	3
102	El Salvador	1.49×10^{10}	31 December 2016 est. [102]	2,400	56
103	Laos	1.198×10^{10}	31 December 2016 est. [103]	1,700	87

List of countries by external debt					
Rank	Country/Region	External debt US dollars	Date	Per capita US dollars	% of GDP
104	Nicaragua	$1.11×10^{10}$	31 December 2016 est. [104]	1,800	83
105	Zimbabwe	$1.09×10^{10}$	31 December 2016 est. [105]	670	77
106	Armenia	$1.0044×10^{10}$	30 June 2017[106]	3,300	94
107	Ivory Coast	$1.00281×10^{10}$	31 December 2015[107]	420	28
108	Cambodia	$9.8244×10^{9}$	31 December 2016[108]	600	49
109	Mozambique	$9.554×10^{9}$	31 December 2016 est. [109]	320	79
110	Zambia	$9.27×10^{9}$	31 December 2016 est. [110]	540	45
111	Albania	$8.6315×10^{9}$	30 June 2017[111]	2,900	73
112	Honduras	$8.042×10^{9}$	31 December 2016 est. [112]	1,000	38
113	Kyrgyzstan	$7.8668×10^{9}$	31 December 2016[113]	1,300	120

List of countries by external debt					
Rank	Country/Region	External debt US dollars	Date	Per capita US dollars	% of GDP
114	Macedonia	7.6455×10^9	31 December 2016[114]	3,700	74
115	Cameroon	7.375×10^9	31 December 2016 est. [115]	300	24
116	Yemen	7.1915×10^9	31 January 2015[116]	260	21
117	Iran	7.116×10^9	31 December 2016 est. [117]	90	2
118	Azerbaijan	6.9132×10^9	31 December 2016[118]	1,300	20
119	Moldova	6.5947×10^9	31 December 2016[119]	1,600	98
120	Namibia	6.515×10^9	31 December 2016 est. [120]	2,500	64
121	Myanmar	6.4012×10^9	31 December 2015[121]	120	17
122	Bolivia	6.3408×10^9	31 December 2015[122]	600	19
123	Uganda	6.241×10^9	31 December 2016 est. [123]	150	24
124	Senegal	6.186×10^9	31 December 2016 est. [124]	390	42

List of countries by external debt					
Rank	Country/Region	External debt US dollars	Date	Per capita US dollars	% of GDP
125	Syria	5.918×10^9	31 December 2016 est. [125]	300	24
126	Democratic Republic of the Congo	5.331×10^9	31 December 2016 est. [126]	70	13
127	Gabon	5.158×10^9	31 December 2016 est. [127]	2,900	35
128	North Korea	5×10^9	2013 est. [128]	200	18
129	Republic of the Congo	4.817×10^9	31 December 2016 est. [129]	1,000	55
130	Bosnia and Herzegovina	4.7166×10^9	30 June 2017 [130]	1,300	31
131	Barbados	4.49×10^9	2010 est. [131]	15,700	100
132	Madagascar	4.007×10^9	31 December 2016 est. [132]	160	41
133	Mali	3.626×10^9	31 December 2016 est. [133]	200	26

List of countries by external debt					
Rank	Country/Region	External debt US dollars	Date	Per capita US dollars	% of GDP
134	Mauritania	3.585×10^9	31 December 2016 est. [134]	840	76
135	Libya	3.531×10^9	31 December 2016 est. [135]	550	9
136	Nepal	3.4502×10^9	31 July 2015[136]	120	16
137	Algeria	3.139×10^9	30 June 2016[137]	80	2
138	Burkina Faso	3.092×10^9	31 December 2016 est. [138]	160	26
139	Somalia	3.054×10^9	31 December 2013 est. [139]	270	52
140	Niger	2.729×10^9	31 December 2016 est. [140]	130	36
141	Montenegro	2.64×10^9	30 June 2018[141]	4,260	60
142	Seychelles	2.552×10^9	31 December 2016 est. [142]	26,200	180

List of countries by external debt					
Rank	**Country/Region**	**External debt US dollars**	**Date**	**Per capita US dollars**	**% of GDP**
143	Rwanda	2.442×10^9	31 December 2016 est. [143]	200	29
—	Bermuda	2.435×10^9	2015 est. [144]	39,700	47
—	Kosovo	2.3897×10^9	30 June 2017 [145]	1,200	34
144	Benin	2.34×10^9	31 December 2016 est. [146]	200	26
145	Tajikistan	2.2741×10^9	31 December 2016 [147]	260	35
146	Bhutan	2.261×10^9	31 December 2016 est. [148]	2,900	108
147	Haiti	2.022×10^9	31 December 2016 est. [149]	180	24
148	Malawi	1.921×10^9	31 December 2016 est. [150]	100	35
149	Chad	1.875×10^9	31 December 2016 est. [151]	130	18
150	Botswana	1.6854×10^9	31 March 2017 [152]	720	10

List of countries by external debt

Rank	Country/Region	External debt US dollars	Date	Per capita US dollars	% of GDP
—	Palestine	$1.662×10^9$	31 March 2016 est. [153]	340	17
151	Cape Verde	$1.66×10^9$	31 December 2016 est. [154]	3,100	99
152	Sierra Leone	$1.561×10^9$	31 December 2016 est. [155]	230	36
153	Equatorial Guinea	$1.364×10^9$	31 December 2016 est. [156]	1,500	12
154	Djibouti	$1.339×10^9$	31 December 2016 est. [157]	1,500	71
155	Guinea	$1.332×10^9$	31 December 2016 est. [158]	100	20
156	Belize	$1.327×10^9$	31 December 2016 est. [159]	3,500	75
157	Afghanistan	$1.28×10^9$	FY-2010/11 [160]	40	7
158	Suriname	$1.235×10^9$	31 December 2016 est. [161]	2,200	30

List of countries by external debt					
Rank	Country/Region	External debt US dollars	Date	Per capita US dollars	% of GDP
159	Togo	$1.173×10^9$	31 December 2016 est. [162]	150	26
160	Guyana	$1.143×10^9$	31 December 2015[163]	1,500	36
161	Liberia	$1.111×10^9$	31 December 2016 est. [164]	230	51
162	Guinea-Bissau	$1.095×10^9$	31 December 2010 est. [165]	570	94
163	Lesotho	948,800,000	31 December 2016 est. [166]	430	53
—	*Faroe Islands*	888,800,000	2010[167]	18,400	38
164	Fiji	833,400,000	31 December 2016 est. [168]	900	18
165	Eritrea	820,200,000	31 December 2016 est. [169]	150	15
166	Maldives	741,600,000	2014 est.[170]	2,000	23

List of countries by external debt					
Rank	Country/Region	External debt US dollars	Date	Per capita US dollars	% of GDP
167	Burundi	705,200,000	31 December 2016 est. [171]	60	26
—	Aruba	693,200,000	31 December 2014 est. [172]	6,600	28
168	Central African Republic	686,900,000	31 December 2016 est. [173]	130	39
169	Grenada	679,000,000	2013 est. [174]	6,300	66
170	The Gambia	541,800,000	31 December 2016 est. [175]	260	61
171	Saint Lucia	513,200,000	31 December 2016 est. [176]	2,700	36
172	Turkmenistan	502,800,000	31 December 2016 est. [177]	90	1
173	Solomon Islands	491,500,000	31 December 2013 est. [178]	800	40
174	Swaziland	470,500,000	31 December 2016 est. [179]	360	14

	List of countries by external debt				
Rank	Country/Region	External debt US dollars	Date	Per capita US dollars	% of GDP
175	Samoa	447,200,000	31 December 2013 est. [180]	2,300	51
176	Antigua and Barbuda	441,200,000	31 December 2012[181]	4,700	34
177	Saint Vincent and the Grenadines	321,100,000	31 December 2016 est. [182]	2,900	42
178	Timor-Leste	311,500,000	31 December 2014 est. [183]	250	12
179	Dominica	288,600,000	31 December 2016 est. [184]	3,900	55
—	Cook Islands	281,200,000	31 December 2011[185]	13,400	23
180	Sao Tome and Principe	236,500,000	31 December 2016 est. [186]	1,200	67
181	Tonga	233,100,000	31 December 2016 est. [187]	2,200	54
182	Vanuatu	208,100,000	31 December 2016 est. [188]	750	27

List of countries by external debt					
Rank	Country/Region	External debt US dollars	Date	Per capita US dollars	% of GDP
183	Saint Kitts and Nevis	187,500,000	31 December 2016 est. [189]	3,300	20
184	Comoros	133,300,000	31 December 2016 est. [190]	160	21
—	New Caledonia	112,000,000	31 December 2013 est. [191]	420	1
185	Marshall Islands	97,960,000	2013 est. [192]	1,800	52
186	Federated States of Micronesia	93,600,000	2013 est. [193]	900	29
—	Cayman Islands	79,000,000	1998 est.	2,100	7
—	Greenland	36,400,000	2010 [194]	650	2
187	Nauru	33,300,000	2004 est. [195]	3,200	22
—	British Virgin Islands	17,670,000	31 December 2016 [196]	570	2
188	Kiribati	13,600,000	2013 est. [197]	120	8

List of countries by external debt					
Rank	Country/Region	External debt US dollars	Date	Per capita US dollars	% of GDP
—	Anguilla	8,800,000	1998[198]	590	5
—	Wallis and Futuna	3,670,000	2004[199]	280	6
—	Montserrat	1,040,000	31 December 2011[200]	200	2
189	Brunei	0	2014[201]	0	0
190	Liechtenstein	0	2001[202]	0	0
—	Macau	0	31 December 2013[203]	0	0
—	Niue	0	27 October 2016[204]	0	0
191	Andorra		N/A		
192	San Marino	352,000,000	2016[205]	10,604	22.5
193	South Sudan		N/A		
194	Tuvalu		N/A		

References

1. *"CEIC Data"*. CEIC. Retrieved 2019-05-02.

2. *"Office for National Statistics"*. ONS. Retrieved 2018-04-04.

3. *"Banque de France"*. Retrieved 2018-04-04.

4. *"Deutsche Bundesbank"* (PDF). Retrieved 2018-04-04.

5. *"De Nederlandsche Bank"*. Retrieved 2018-04-04.

6. *"Banque Centrale du Luxembourg"*. Retrieved 2018-04-04.

7. *"Ministry of Finance Japan"*. Retrieved 2018-04-04.

8. *"Euromoney Institutional Investor Company"*. Retrieved 2018-04-04.

9. *"The World Factbook"* (PDF). Retrieved 2018-04-04.

10. *"Statistics Canada"*. Retrieved 2018-04-04.

11. *https://cn.reuters.com/article/china-safe-march-foreign-debt-0629-idCNKBS1JP1CR*

12. *"Euromoney Institutional Investor Company"*. Retrieved 2018-04-04.

13. *"Australian Bureau of Statistics"*. Retrieved 2017-07-09.

14. *"Statistics Singapore"*. Retrieved 2017-09-30.

15. *"National Bank of Belgium"*. NBB. Retrieved 2017-09-30.

16. *"Census and Statistics Department of Hong Kong"*.

17. *"Euromoney Institutional Investor Company"*. Retrieved 2017-09-30.

18. *"Oesterreichische NationalBank"*. Retrieved 2017-09-30.

19. *"Euromoney Institutional Investor Company"*. Retrieved 2017-09-17.

20. *"Banco Central do Brasil"*. BCB. Retrieved 2017-11-04.

21. *http://www.cbr.ru/eng/statistics/?Prtid=svs*

22. *"India's External Debt Rises By 12% To Over $529 Billion"*. Retrieved 2018-07-07.

23. *"Danmarks Nationalbank"*. Retrieved 2017-09-30.

24. *"Euromoney Institutional Investor Company"*. Retrieved 2017-09-30.

25. *"Bank of Greece"*. Retrieved 2018-04-04.

26. *"T.C. Başbakanlık Hazine Müsteşarlığı"*. Retrieved 2018-04-04.

27. *"Euromoney Institutional Investor Company"*. Retrieved 2017-09-30.

28. *"Sistema de Informacion Economica"*. Retrieved 2018-04-04.

29. *"Euromoney Institutional Investor Company"*. Retrieved 2017-09-30.

30. *"Narodowy Bank Polski"*. Retrieved 2017-09-30.

31. *"Bank Indonesia"*. Retrieved 2017-09-30.

32. *"Euromoney Institutional Investor Company"*. Retrieved 2018-08-20.

33. *"Statista"*. Retrieved 2019-01-13.

34. *"The World Factbook"*. CIA. Central Intelligence Agency. Retrieved 2017-05-07.

35. *"The World Factbook"*. CIA. Central Intelligence Agency. Retrieved 2017-05-07.

36. *"Observatorio Fiscal Federal"*. Retrieved 2017-05-06.

37. *"Euromoney Institutional Investor Company"*. Retrieved 2017-09-17.

38. *"Central Bank of the Republic of China (TAIWAN)"* (PDF). Retrieved 2018-08-20.

39. *"Euromoney Institutional Investor Company"*. Retrieved 2017-07-09.

40. *"Euromoney Institutional Investor Company"*. Retrieved 2018-08-20.

41. *"Euromoney Institutional Investor Company"*. Retrieved 2017-08-06.

42. *"The World Factbook"*. CIA. Central Intelligence Agency. Retrieved 2017-05-07.

43. *"Statistics - External Debt"*. Bank of Thailand.

44. *"Euromoney Institutional Investor Company"*. Retrieved 2017-09-30.

45. *"Euromoney Institutional Investor Company"*. Retrieved 2017-05-06.

46. *"Czech National Bank"*. Retrieved 2017-04-30.

47. *"Euromoney Institutional Investor Company"*. Retrieved 2017-05-06.

48. *"Euromoney Institutional Investor Company"*. Retrieved 2017-09-30.

49. *"Euromoney Institutional Investor Company"*. Retrieved 2017-09-30.

50. *"Euromoney Institutional Investor Company"*. Retrieved 2017-05-06.

51. *"Euromoney Institutional Investor Company"*. Retrieved 2017-07-09.

52. *"Euromoney Institutional Investor Company"*. Retrieved 2017-09-30.

53. *"The Express Tribune > Business Pakistan's external debt soars to record $91.8b"*. Retrieved 2018-05-30.

54. *"Bank Of Israel"*. Retrieved 2017-06-30.

55. *"Euromoney Institutional Investor Company"*. Retrieved 2017-09-30.

56. *"Euromoney Institutional Investor Company"*. Retrieved 2017-05-06.

57. *"Euromoney Institutional Investor Company"*. Retrieved 2017-07-17.

58. *"The World Factbook"*. CIA. Central Intelligence Agency. Retrieved 2017-05-07.

59. *"Euromoney Institutional Investor Company"*. Retrieved 2017-05-06.

60. *"Euromoney Institutional Investor Company"*. Retrieved 2017-09-30.

61. *"Euromoney Institutional Investor Company"*. Retrieved 2017-09-30.

62. *"Euromoney Institutional Investor Company"*. Retrieved 2017-09-30.

63. *"The World Factbook"*. CIA. Central Intelligence Agency. Retrieved 2017-05-07.

64. *"Euromoney Institutional Investor Company"*. Retrieved 2017-05-06.

65. *"Euromoney Institutional Investor Company"*. Retrieved 2017-09-30.

66. *"Euromoney Institutional Investor Company"*. Retrieved 2017-05-06.

67. *"Euromoney Institutional Investor Company"*. Retrieved 2017-09-30.

68. *"Bulgarian National Bank"*. Retrieved 2018-04-04.

69. *"Euromoney Institutional Investor Company"*. Retrieved 2017-05-06.

70. *"The World Factbook"*. CIA. Central Intelligence Agency. Retrieved 2017-05-07.

71. *"Euromoney Institutional Investor Company"*. Retrieved 2017-11-04.

72. *"Euromoney Institutional Investor Company"*. Retrieved 2017-09-30.

73. *"Euromoney   Institutional   Investor   Company"*. Retrieved 2017-09-30.

74. *"Euromoney   Institutional   Investor   Company"*. Retrieved 2017-05-06.

75. *"Euromoney   Institutional   Investor   Company"*. Retrieved 2017-09-30.

76. *"The World Factbook"*. CIA. Central Intelligence Agency. Retrieved 2017-05-07.

77. *"Euromoney   Institutional   Investor   Company"*. Retrieved 2017-05-06.

78. *"The World Factbook"*. CIA. Central Intelligence Agency. Retrieved 2017-05-07.

79. *"Euromoney   Institutional   Investor   Company"*. Retrieved 2017-05-06.

80. *"Euromoney   Institutional   Investor   Company"*. Retrieved 2017-09-17.

81. *"Euromoney   Institutional   Investor   Company"*. Retrieved 2017-05-06.

82. *"The World Factbook"*. CIA. Central Intelligence Agency. Retrieved 2017-05-07.

83. *"Euromoney   Institutional   Investor   Company"*. Retrieved 2017-09-30.

84. *"The World Factbook"*. CIA. Central Intelligence Agency. Retrieved 2017-05-07.

85. *"Euromoney   Institutional   Investor   Company"*. Retrieved 2017-09-30.

86. *"The World Factbook"*. CIA. Central Intelligence Agency. Retrieved 2017-05-07.

87. *"Central Bank of Trinidad & Tobago"*. Retrieved 2017-05-13.

88. *"The World Factbook"*. CIA. Central Intelligence Agency. Retrieved 2017-05-07.

89. *"The World Factbook"*. CIA. Central Intelligence Agency. Retrieved 2017-05-07.

90. *"The World Factbook"*. CIA. Central Intelligence Agency. Retrieved 2017-04-30.

91. *"Euromoney Institutional Investor Company"*. Retrieved 2017-05-06.

92. *"The World Factbook"*. CIA. Central Intelligence Agency. Retrieved 2017-05-07.

93. *"The World Factbook"*. CIA. Central Intelligence Agency. Retrieved 2017-05-06.

94. *"Euromoney Institutional Investor Company"*. Retrieved 2018-04-04.

95. *"The World Factbook"*. CIA. Central Intelligence Agency. Retrieved 2017-05-07.

96. *"The World Factbook"*. CIA. Central Intelligence Agency. Retrieved 2017-05-07.

97. *"Euromoney Institutional Investor Company"*. Retrieved 2017-05-06.

98. *"Euromoney Institutional Investor Company"*. Retrieved 2017-05-06.

99. *"The World Factbook"*. CIA. Central Intelligence Agency. Retrieved 2017-05-07.

100. *"The World Factbook"*. CIA. Central Intelligence Agency. Retrieved 2017-04-09.

101. *"Euromoney Institutional Investor Company"*. Retrieved 2017-05-06.

102. *"The World Factbook"*. CIA. Central Intelligence Agency. Retrieved 2017-05-07.

103. *"The World Factbook"*. CIA. Central Intelligence Agency. Retrieved 2017-05-07.

104. *"The World Factbook"*. CIA. Central Intelligence Agency. Retrieved 2017-05-07.

105. *"The World Factbook"*. CIA. Central Intelligence Agency. Retrieved 2017-04-08.

106. *"Euromoney Institutional Investor Company"*. Retrieved 2017-05-06.

107. *"Euromoney Institutional Investor Company"*. Retrieved 2017-05-06.

108. *"Euromoney Institutional Investor Company"*. Retrieved 2017-05-06.

109. *The World Factbook"*. CIA. Central Intelligence Agency. Retrieved 2017-05-07.

110. *"The World Factbook"*. CIA. Central Intelligence Agency. Retrieved 2017-05-07.

111. *"Euromoney Institutional Investor Company"*. Retrieved 2017-09-30.

112. *"The World Factbook"*. CIA. Central Intelligence Agency. Retrieved 2017-05-07.

113. *"Euromoney Institutional Investor Company"*. Retrieved 2017-05-06.

114. *"Euromoney Institutional Investor Company"*. Retrieved 2017-05-06.

115. *"The World Factbook"*. CIA. Central Intelligence Agency. Retrieved 2017-05-07.

116. *"Euromoney Institutional Investor Company"*. Retrieved 2017-05-06.

117. *"The World Factbook"*. CIA. Central Intelligence Agency. Retrieved 2017-04-09.

118. *"Euromoney Institutional Investor Company"*. Retrieved 2017-05-06.

119. *"Euromoney Institutional Investor Company"*. Retrieved 2017-05-06.

120. *"The World Factbook"*. CIA. Central Intelligence Agency. Retrieved 2017-05-07.

121. *"Euromoney Institutional Investor Company"*. Retrieved 2017-05-06.

122. *"Euromoney Institutional Investor Company"*. Retrieved 2017-05-06.

123. *"The World Factbook"*. CIA. Central Intelligence Agency. Retrieved 2017-05-07.

124. *"The World Factbook"*. CIA. Central Intelligence Agency. Retrieved 2017-05-07.

125. *The World Factbook"*. CIA. Central Intelligence Agency. Retrieved 2017-05-07.

126. *"The World Factbook"*. CIA. Central Intelligence Agency. Retrieved 2017-04-08.

127. *"The World Factbook"*. CIA. Central Intelligence Agency. Retrieved 2017-05-07.

128. *"The World Factbook"*. CIA. Central Intelligence Agency. Retrieved 2017-05-07.

129. *"The World Factbook"*. CIA. Central Intelligence Agency. Retrieved 2017-04-08.

130. *"Euromoney Institutional Investor Company"*. Retrieved 2017-09-30.

131. *"The World Factbook"*. CIA. Central Intelligence Agency. Retrieved 2017-05-07.

132. *"The World Factbook"*. CIA. Central Intelligence Agency. Retrieved 2017-05-07.

133. *"The World Factbook"*. CIA. Central Intelligence Agency. Retrieved 2017-05-07.

134. *"The World Factbook"*. CIA. Central Intelligence Agency. Retrieved 2017-05-07.

135. *"The World Factbook"*. CIA. Central Intelligence Agency. Retrieved 2017-05-07.

136. *"Euromoney Institutional Investor Company"*. Retrieved 2017-05-06.

137. *"Euromoney Institutional Investor Company"*. Retrieved 2017-05-06.

138. *"The World Factbook"*. CIA. Central Intelligence Agency. Retrieved 2017-05-07.

139. *"The World Factbook"*. CIA. Central Intelligence Agency. Retrieved 2017-04-07.

140. *"The World Factbook"*. CIA. Central Intelligence Agency. Retrieved 2017-05-07.

141. *"Euromoney Institutional Investor Company"*. Retrieved 2018-06-30.

142. *The World Factbook"*. CIA. Central Intelligence Agency. Retrieved 2017-05-07.

143. *"The World Factbook"*. CIA. Central Intelligence Agency. Retrieved 2017-05-07.

144. *"The World Factbook"*. CIA. Central Intelligence Agency. Retrieved 2017-05-07.

145. *"Euromoney Institutional Investor Company"*. Retrieved 2017-09-30.

146. *"The World Factbook"*. CIA. Central Intelligence Agency. Retrieved 2017-05-07.

147. *"Euromoney Institutional Investor Company"*. Retrieved 2017-05-06.

148. *"The World Factbook"*. CIA. Central Intelligence Agency. Retrieved 2017-05-06.

149. *"The World Factbook"*. CIA. Central Intelligence Agency. Retrieved 2017-05-07.

150. *"The World Factbook"*. CIA. Central Intelligence Agency. Retrieved 2017-04-07.

151. *"The World Factbook"*. CIA. Central Intelligence Agency. Retrieved 2017-04-07.

152. *"Euromoney Institutional Investor Company"*. Retrieved 2017-05-06.

153. *"The World Factbook"*. CIA. Central Intelligence Agency. Retrieved 2017-04-07.

154. *"The World Factbook"*. CIA. Central Intelligence Agency. Retrieved 2017-05-07.

155. *"The World Factbook"*. CIA. Central Intelligence Agency. Retrieved 2017-05-07.

156. *"The World Factbook"*. CIA. Central Intelligence Agency. Retrieved 2017-05-07.

157. *"The World Factbook"*. CIA. Central Intelligence Agency. Retrieved 2017-05-07.

158. *"The World Factbook"*. CIA. Central Intelligence Agency. Retrieved 2017-05-07.

159. *"The World Factbook"*. CIA. Central Intelligence Agency. Retrieved 2017-05-07.

160. *"The World Factbook"*. CIA. Central Intelligence Agency. Retrieved 2017-05-07.

161. *"The World Factbook"*. CIA. Central Intelligence Agency. Retrieved 2017-05-07.

162. *"The World Factbook"*. CIA. Central Intelligence Agency. Retrieved 2017-05-07.

163. *"Caribbean Development Bank"* (PDF). Retrieved 2017-08-11.

164. *"The World Factbook"*. CIA. Central Intelligence Agency. Retrieved 2017-05-07.

165. *"The World Factbook"*. CIA. Central Intelligence Agency. Retrieved 2017-05-07.

166. *"The World Factbook"*. CIA. Central Intelligence Agency. Retrieved 2017-05-07.

167. *"The World Factbook"*. CIA. Central Intelligence Agency. Retrieved 2017-05-07.

168. *"The World Factbook"*. CIA. Central Intelligence Agency. Retrieved 2017-04-07.

169. *"The World Factbook"*. CIA. Central Intelligence Agency. Retrieved 2017-05-07.

170. *"The World Factbook"*. CIA. Central Intelligence Agency. Retrieved 2017-05-07.

171. *"The World Factbook"*. CIA. Central Intelligence Agency. Retrieved 2017-04-07.

172. *"The World Factbook"*. CIA. Central Intelligence Agency. Retrieved 2017-05-07.

173. *"The World Factbook"*. CIA. Central Intelligence Agency. Retrieved 2017-05-07.

174. *"The World Factbook"*. CIA. Central Intelligence Agency. Retrieved 2017-05-07.

175. *"The World Factbook"*. CIA. Central Intelligence Agency. Retrieved 2017-05-07.

176. *"The World Factbook"*. CIA. Central Intelligence Agency. Retrieved 2017-05-07.

177. *"The World Factbook"*. CIA. Central Intelligence Agency. Retrieved 2017-05-07.

178. *"The World Factbook"*. CIA. Central Intelligence Agency. Retrieved 2017-05-07.

179. *"The World Factbook"*. CIA. Central Intelligence Agency. Retrieved 2017-05-07.

180. *"The World Factbook"*. CIA. Central Intelligence Agency. Retrieved 2017-05-07.

181. *"The World Factbook"*. CIA. Central Intelligence Agency. Retrieved 2017-05-07.

182. *"The World Factbook"*. CIA. Central Intelligence Agency. Retrieved 2017-05-07.

183. *"The World Factbook"*. CIA. Central Intelligence Agency. Retrieved 2017-05-07.

184. *"The World Factbook"*. CIA. Central Intelligence Agency. Retrieved 2017-05-07.

185. *"Asian Development Bank"* (PDF). ADB. Asian Development Bank. Retrieved 2017-08-11.

186. *"The World Factbook"*. CIA. Central Intelligence Agency. Retrieved 2017-05-07.

187. *"The World Factbook"*. CIA. Central Intelligence Agency. Retrieved 2017-05-07.

188. *"The World Factbook"*. CIA. Central Intelligence Agency. Retrieved 2017-05-07.

189. *"The World Factbook"*. CIA. Central Intelligence Agency. Retrieved 2017-05-07.

190. *"The World Factbook"*. CIA. Central Intelligence Agency. Retrieved 2017-05-07.

191. *"The World Factbook"*. CIA. Central Intelligence Agency. Retrieved 2017-05-07.

192. *"The World Factbook"*. CIA. Central Intelligence Agency. Retrieved 2017-05-07.

193. *"The World Factbook"*. CIA. Central Intelligence Agency. Retrieved 2017-05-07.

194. *"The World Factbook"*. CIA. Central Intelligence Agency. Retrieved 2017-05-07.

195. *"The World Factbook"*. CIA. Central Intelligence Agency. Retrieved 2017-05-07.

196. *"Government of the Virgin Islands"*. Retrieved 2017-05-13.

197. *"The World Factbook"*. CIA. Central Intelligence Agency. Retrieved 2017-05-07.

198. *"The World Factbook"*. CIA. Central Intelligence Agency. Retrieved 2017-05-07.

199. *"The World Factbook"*. CIA. Central Intelligence Agency. Retrieved 2017-05-07.

200. *"Caribbean Development Bank"* (PDF). Retrieved 2017-08-11.

201.   *"The World Factbook"*. CIA. Central Intelligence Agency. Retrieved 2017-05-07.

202.   *"The World Factbook"*. CIA. Central Intelligence Agency. Retrieved 2017-05-07.

203.   *"The World Factbook"*. CIA. Central Intelligence Agency. Retrieved 2017-05-07.

204.   *"The Guardian"*. The Guardian. The Guardian. Retrieved 2016-10-27.

205.   *"San Marino National Debt 2016"*. countryeconomy.com. Retrieved 2019-01-15.

Bibliography

Ovcaricek-Rostok I. *The Economic Success of a State: The Principle of Economic Duals and Category of Diversified Money.* Houston: Strategic Book Publishing and Rights Co., 2013.

Ovcaricek-Rostok I. *Debts of the State and the Danger of Economic Collapse.* Houston: Strategic Book Publishing and Rights Co., 2014., p.94.

Ovcaricek-Rostok I. *Optimum in the Economics of a State.* Houston: Strategic Book Publishing and Rights Co., 2015.

Ovcaricek-Rostok I. *The Gold Money Constant and Entrepreneurship.* Houston: Strategic Book Publishing and Rights Co., 2016.

List of Tables

List of Schemes

Author Biography

Ivan Ovcaricek-Rostok was born in Croatia. He attended the University of Zagreb and obtained both Master and Doctor of Science degrees in Economics.

After finishing his studies, he began working as an economic analyst and later as manager of economic and technical services for a large industrial company. From 1967 to 1989, Ivan worked in several positions, including factory director and assistant to a principal director for economy for a large joint company.

Ivan has written and published forty-five professional and scientific papers in the field of economics and traveled on professional study tours to London, Moscow, Paris, Munich, and Stockholm.

Appendix

(1)

The idealistic policy of a free world trade brought the United States almost to the financial collapse. How to solve this problem, is the application of the category of diversified money in the US foreign trade.

(2)

The purchasing power of the economic space of the US is the largest economic resource in the world that free of charge is used and exploited by a large number of partner countries.

(3)

Introducing customs is the method of the 20th century. The new method of diversified money is economically civilized and objectivated.

(4)

The size of the purchasing power of the economic space of the US is one-quarter of all the world's resources.

(5)

The Import of the U.S. from individual countries should be of the same value as the exports to that countries. That's "Conditio sine qua non". Without this the foreign trade with the U.S. is not fair.

(6)

The average monthly salary in the US is $ 4,670, and in China it is $ 601 or less than in the US by 7.8 times. In such conditions, the concept of free trade between the US and China is just nonsense. The solution to this problem is the balanced trade through diversified money.

(7)

The concept of free foreign trade brings to the US an annual financial loss the estimated magnitude of which is $ 1000 billion. This can only be solved by introducing diversified money in that trade. In this way, elements of economic honesty and equality are introduced.

(8)

According to the final data, the external debt of U.S. for 2017 and 2018, was reduced from an annual average growth of 9.6% to 2.7% or 3.6 times, and the economic security quotient was raised from 0.26 to 1.69 or 6.5 times. These are the best results for the past 57 years.

(9)

By introducing Diversified Money into Foreign Trade the US generates an annual GDP growth within 10 to 15 years in the amount of 4 to 6% as well as strengthening of broad technological development in production. In addition, there is also the growth of the general level of wealth.

(10)

If it comes to a balanced foreign trade of the US with its partner countries as a result of the introduction of diversified money, for the partner states that would be a serious economic challenge, because balanced trade is the basic form of fighting against the economic crisis.

(11)

The annual production value of the US is less than the annual consumption value of about $1000 billion. This deviation gradually generates an economic crisis. These two categories should be balanced by increasing exports or reducing imports. An old debt remains.

(12)

If the US immediately does not start to solve the problem of its external debt, it could grow to such a size that it will never be able to repay it. The result would be the radical impoverishment of the state and the population, and the loss of the present international status.

(13)

The current US Gross debt of $ 22 trillion or 35% of the world GDP of one year is the biggest problem in modern economic history. It is threatening to create a world economic catastrophe.

(14)

The only realistic possibility for the US to repay its catastrophically large external debt of $ 22 trillion, within 10 to 20 years, is the application of the concept of diversified money in foreign trade. Everything else is an illusion.

(15)

Historically and strictly mathematically, the concept of free international trade is an economic mistake. Evidence for this is the catastrophic size of US foreign debt. This concept needs to be replaced by economic equilibrium and corrected by economic aid.

(16)

Excessive debts of developed states can produce the effect of egalitarian syndrome. This means turning these countries into economically poor, for a large debt repayment. It's an economic reversal.

(17)

Gross debt as percentage of GDP Unites States and index
2007   62 %   100
2010   92 %   148
2011   102 % 165
2018   108 % 174

(18)

The US is the world's spine of economy. That's why this economy needs to be healthy and an example. The present big external debt is a cancer on that body.

....

Twitter: Nov 2018, May 2019.

Review Requested:

If you loved this book, would you please provide
a review at Amazon.com?